The Prince and the Nanny

Odell M. Bjerkness

The Prince and the Nanny

The Life of Prince Harald, now King of Norway,
as told in Historical Context and
through the Journal of his Nurse, Inga Berg

Odell M. Bjerkness

SKANDISK INC.

Skandisk, Inc.
6667 West Old Shakopee Rd., Suite 109
Bloomington, Minnesota 55438-2622
www.skandisk.com

©2008, 2009 by Odell M. Bjerkness
First edition published 2008. Second edition 2009

Design: Bill Lundborg/West44th Street Graphics
Revised Cover Design: Kirsten Sevig

Library of Congress Control Number: 2009925590

ISBN 10: 1-57534-076-3
ISBN 13: 978-1-57534-076-0

Printed in the United States of America
13 12 11 10 09   2 3 4 5

Cover photo: During the *Syttende Mai* Parade in Oslo, Norwegian children passed in review before the Royal Family who was standing on the balcony of the Royal Palace.

Inset photo: Nurse Inga Berg and Prince Harald.

Title page photo—from the left: Princess Ragnhild, pediatric nurse Inga Berg, Prince Harald, and Princess Astrid on the terrace of their home at Skaugum.

CONTENTS

PREFACE

My parents, Marie Berg Bjerkness and Olai Jonson Bjerkness, grew up on opposite sides of Norway and then met in Granite Falls, Minnesota. They spoke Norwegian in our home, and there was no doubt that our background was fully Norwegian in language and culture; yet my father and mother were hesitant to discuss the lives and families they had left behind. My mother, with her sister Thea, had emigrated to America in 1912, leaving their 16-year-old sister Inga in Norway to assume the family burdens of caring for the younger siblings and their widowed father. Inga's home duties would be the first of the practical experiences on which she would build a career to be a child's nurse for the Royal Family.

While growing up our family was only faintly aware that my Aunt Inga was a celebrity of sorts back in Norway. I met Inga for the first time in Norway in 1957 and again in 1973. I remember her as much shorter than my mother Marie, just a little over five feet tall, but with a strong British accent, and a poise and confidence that set her apart from the other relatives. She had many questions for me about family members in America, but her past service as a pediatric nurse for Prince Harald did not enter that conversation. Decades later I visited Norway for an extended time. Through newspaper articles I learned of the meticulous *Dagbok* (journal) that Inga kept during her service as the Royal Nanny to the then future King of Norway, Harald V. That journal is the heart of this book.[1]

Inga Berg served as pediatric nurse for Prince Harald for the first year and a half of his life. As a certified children's nurse living in the Norwegian royal household, she was in a unique position to observe and take part in the life of the Royal Family.

Her journal chronicles the young Prince's development. She charts his height and weight, his diet, and his acquisition of new skills. She also describes her everyday experiences with the Royal Family, providing a rare glimpse into the private lives of Crown Prince Olav, Crown Princess Märtha, King Haakon, Queen Maud, Princesses Astrid and Ragnhild, and young Prince Harald.

The journal bears witness to a period of transition in the Norwegian monarchy from a very formal, traditional monarchial lifestyle to the more familiar, unpretentious lifestyle of the modern Norwegian royals. It also gives a portrait of Inga herself, an extraordinary woman for her time who was raised in humble surroundings, overcame adversity, studied to become a nurse, and eventually served in the most prestigious house in Norway to help raise the first prince to be born on Norwegian soil in almost 600 years.

This book is organized in four sections:

▶ Part I provides background information about the life of Inga Berg and the Royal Family.

▶ Part II is Inga's journal from her 18 months at the royal residence at Skaugum, written in Norwegian in her own hand and facing it an English translation with footnotes explaining details in the text.

▶ Part III, the epilogue, completes the story of Prince Harald and Inga Berg, tracing some of the activities of the two families until the present.

▶ The final part of the book contains endnotes, a bibliography, and appendices.

SPECIAL THANKS

My interesting ancestors, relatives and friends made this work possible. Ragnhild Berg, the wife of my cousin Martin Berg, has provided photographs and copies of Inga Berg's journal and access to all of her papers; cousins John and Inger Berg and Marion Berg Balow offered Berg family background information.

I want to thank William H. Halverson, Per Inge and Karin Vik, Jane Dale, and Bjorn Hauge for translation assistance; JoEllen Haugo for indexing; Susan Tapp, Liv Dahl, Laura Boeringa, and Kari and Erik Meyer for proofreading; Nancy Groves, M.D. and John E. Xavier for editorial assistance; Shelly Miller Peters for graphics and initial layout; Bill and Linda Lundborg for layout and design; Arve Ragner, philatelist; Hanna Mai Svaboe of the Norwegian Nurses' Union (*Sykepleierforbund*) for information on Norway's nurses movement; Tove D. Johansen, *Nasjonalbibliotek*, and Leif Thingsrud, *Riksarkivet*, for documentation; Hågen Sætran, Master of the Household at Skaugum, *Det Kongelige Hoff*, for the interview and private tour of Skaugum; and David Smith for assistance in research and for being general editor. My wife, Joann Marie, has been of inestimable assistance in all phases of producing this book.

This book is based on a paper presented at a conference to celebrate the centennial of Norway's independence from Sweden in 1905. The Royal Norwegian Consul General and Norway House, both located in Minneapolis, Minnesota, sponsored the event. The former Consulate (now closed) was the official representative of Norway in the Midwest. Norway House is an organization whose programs provide a bridge between the people of the American Midwest and Norway, and a place where Norwegian-Americans, Norwegians and their friends can gather.

I am very grateful to the many members of the American-born Bjerkness family who have always been supportive of this project. While growing up, all of our children and now our twelve grandchildren have been very curious about the Norwegian relatives whom they never met. Knowing this part of our family history brings all of us closer.

Jeg vil gjerne få takke alle dere som har hjulpet meg med denne boken.

Odell M. Bjerkness
Edina, Minnesota
ojbjerkness@aol.com

For my wife, Joann Marie,
and children Kristian Erik, Kai Christopher, Kari Marie, and Brent Peter

Historical Background
for the Journal

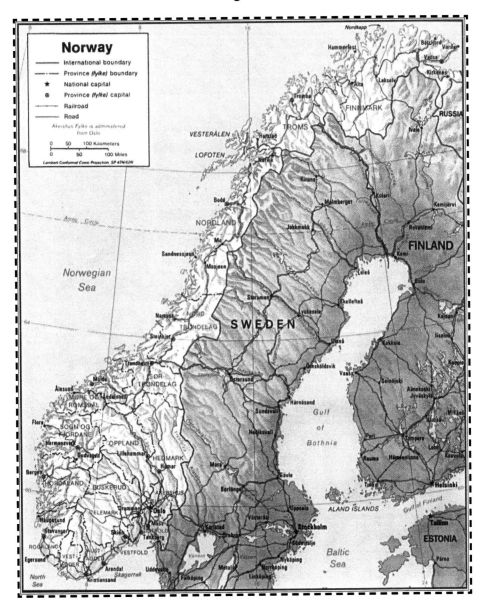

*Topographical map of Norway and Sweden shows the major cities
and administrative districts.*

The families of Prince Harald and Inga Berg can be traced back hundreds of years, Harald to the 800s and Inga to the 1250s. Because of the historical importance of the royal families, detailed records were kept, mainly by clerics. Inga Berg's family had been in the Valdres Valley before the building of the Reinli Stave Church in Bagn in 1250 and church records go back to the 1500s. Her ancestors were farmers, craftsmen and woodsmen; his were leaders, warriors and explorers. Historical context gives a good framework to look at both families.

Momentous Times in 1905

In 1905 the leaders of the Norwegian government sought to reinforce in its citizenry a sense of pride in their history and tradition through the reestablishment of a truly Norwegian constitutional monarchy. The potential future king, Haakon, and three-year-old future crown prince, Olav, were selected from the European royal families.

Although the bloodline of Haakon and Olav was connected to the legendary Viking warrior kings from whom they eventually borrowed new names, most of their immediate ancestors were from the countries that had withheld full autonomy from Norway for almost six centuries. King Haakon VII, a Dane, would be a naturalized monarch who would learn on the job, as best he could, to be Norwegian. Three-year-old Prince Olav's orientation in his new country would be somewhat compromised by his monolingual British mother.

Thirty-one years later Olav and Märtha prepared to raise Harald, the first native-born heir to the new throne in nearly six centuries, to be as Norwegian as possible, despite the fact that he lived with parents and grandparents originally from Sweden, Denmark and England.

The occasion of Prince Harald's baptism was indeed a momentous one for Norway and its modern monarchy. From *Aftenposten* March 31, 1937: The setting was the Chapel of the Royal Palace, Oslo Norway, on the baptism of Prince Harald, heir to the throne of Norway.

'The church was quiet, everybody staring for the first time at the Norwegian prince lying calmly in his mother's arms while his big dark eyes were looking straight ahead, a captivating and spellbinding image of the future King of Norway. The Bishop of Oslo summarized his message by saying, "God has once again shown his kindness towards us." The grandfather, King Haakon, addressed the luncheon that followed: "We are allowed to say that the occurrence is of historical significance...It has been 566 years since a Norwegian prince was born in this country and it is a great joy to me that you have received an heir to the position to which I was called 31 years ago.'[2]

Inga Berg's Challenges and Aspirations

For the first year and a half of Prince Harald's life, his live-in pediatric nurse, Inga Berg, spent 24 hours a day with him. She thus had an important influence on his development. Inga's childhood in a rural village northwest of Oslo was typical of childhood in working-class Norway at that time. The death of her mother when Inga was 11 years old burdened her with family responsibilities, requiring her to hone skills in organization and in managing herself and others. Young Inga aspired to a career in children's nursing. Formal training in Oslo and abroad gave her language skills, professional expertise, worldliness, and poise. During more than a decade of professional service to Oslo's well-to-do families, Inga built a reputation that caught the attention of the Royal Family.

History of the Norwegian Monarchies

VIKING KINGS

Almost 10,000 years ago the Ice Age glaciers retreated and seasonal hunters and fishermen came to the land that would be Norway. Norway (literally "the way north") is part of a mountain range on the northwestern edge of Europe that rises from the Atlantic, resulting in 1,645 miles of steep outer coastline, 150,000 islands, and *fjords* that penetrate up to 120 miles inland.

Four or five thousand years passed, hunters became settlers and agriculture started in the southeastern *Oslofjorden* region. Less than three percent of Norway's land was fit for farming, and as the more accessible part was populated, farm settlements appeared farther and farther north along the narrow western coast.

By the sixth century C.E., population pressures led to the formation of tribal trading and defensive groups. Farms were clustered around villages which were joined in larger groups under the leadership of *jarls* (earls). Petty-kings contested for dominion over the *jarls*. In the year 890, the powerful Harald *Hårfagre* (Fair-haired) succeeded in unifying enough territory to have himself considered the first king of all Norway, King Harald I.[3]

During the Viking era (800-1130 C.E.) fishing and farming continued as principal occupations, but shipbuilding also became established to support ventures of exploration, trade and plunder. Norwegian Vikings on fast and well-constructed ships sailed west to the Shetland Islands; the British Isles; the coast of Scotland, including the other nearby islands: the Hebrides, Isle of Man, Orkneys; and into Ireland, where they founded Dublin.

The coronation of King Haakon Håkonsson (Haakon IV–1204-1263) on July 29, 1247, in Christ Church, Bergen is pictured on a commemorative stamp designed by Anne-Mai Solheim. Under Haakon IV's reign Norway enjoyed a golden age with its control extending as far as Greenland and Iceland and other areas including the Faroes, Orkneys, Hebrides and the Shetland Islands.

They later settled Iceland and Greenland, from which in the year 1000, 500 years before the voyages of Columbus, Leif Eriksson sailed to Labrador and to Newfoundland. In 1961, archeologist and explorer, Helge and Anne Stine Ingestad, discovered in Newfoundland the remains of a Viking village at *L'Anse aux Meadows*, the first known settlement of Europeans in the Americas.

NORWAY AND SWEDEN

Norway shared a landmass and a long frontier with Sweden, but dense untracked forests and a spine of formidable mountains separated the two. In contrast to Norway's steep, narrow and wind-swept Atlantic face, Sweden on the leeward side of the mountain range was blessed with more than nine major rivers that irrigated significant farmland on the Gulf of Bothnia. The Swedish Vikings primarily focused attention on Baltic neighbors Finland, Estonia, and Russia, and they used the Volga and Dnieper Rivers as pathways south to the Mediterranean.[4]

NORWAY AND DENMARK

Geopolitics influenced national action for Norway. Its maritime connections were greater to Denmark than to Sweden. The Norwegian Vikings joined forces with the Danes more often than with the Swedes and together they raided, traded, and founded settlements in England, Ireland, Scotland, Frisia (Netherlands), France, and Spain.

Viking leadership of consolidated forces shifted back and forth and was usually determined by elements of physical prowess, skill in sailing, and force of personality, but often by individual wealth used to buy loyalty. Viking leaders like Harald *Hårfagre* also applied any and all of these to consolidate power back in Norway. Depending on their perceived self-interest, Norwegians might direct loyalty toward a leader who was an original countryman or a Dane. This situation continued throughout and after the Viking era.

CHRISTIANITY IN NORWAY

Contact with Christian Europe led to an often brutal religious transformation that expedited Norwegian national unification. Over time the Norse pagan religion was displaced by Roman Catholic Christianity, imported from Britain and mainland Europe by Vikings and missionaries.

Two kings who were instrumental in the change and lent their names to royal tradition were Haakon the Good (Haakon I) 976-995, and Olav Trygvasson (Olav I) 995-1000. Haakon VII and Olav V took their names from these two early kings. A third Christian king, Olav Haraldsson (Olav II) 1015-1028, also brought missionaries from England to Norway and consolidated his power, burned the pagan temples and disrupted the peerage system.

An illumination from *Flateyjarbók* (The Book of Flatey–1387-1390) depicted the death of St. Olav at Stiklestad.

Those practices earned him enemies who sided with a Danish noble and eventually drove Olav into exile in Russia. He returned in 1030, leading an army of Swedish supporters in an attempt to regain his throne. His Danish deposer again rallied Norwegians against Olav, who was defeated and slain at the Battle of Stiklestad (near Trondheim).

One year and five days after his death, the Church in Rome declared Olav a martyr and a saint of the Christian unification of Norway. Pilgrims from all of Northern Europe flocked to his burial site in Trondheim. The seat of the Norwegian archdiocese and the magnificent Gothic Cathedral of Nidaros took root on that spot. The power of the state church made Trondheim an early center of government control in Christian Norway.

THE KALMAR UNION

Geographic separations reinforced cultural distinctions, but Danish, Norwegian, and Swedish traditions remained similar, and the languages remained mutually intelligible. Royal intermarriage strengthened alliances.

During her reign from 1387-1412, Danish-Norwegian-Swedish Queen Margrethe I joined the three countries into the Kalmar Union, named after the Swedish town of Kalmar. In 1450 another treaty was signed by Norway and Denmark that was intended to ensure equality of the two countries and the authority of a Norwegian council over the selection of leaders in that country. Despite written agreements, the monarchy of Denmark continued to use a number of means to impose more control over Norway and Sweden. Sweden extricated itself from the Kalmar Union in 1523 after a Danish purge of noblemen in Stockholm sparked a successful Swedish revolt led by Gustavus Vasa.

In 1536 King Christian III of Denmark abruptly cancelled Norway's autonomy. The next year, in another move to undermine Norwegian nationalism and the power of the Catholic Church, he proclaimed Evangelical Lutheranism the official religion of Denmark and Norway. Until that time, two decades after Martin Luther's theses of 1517, the German Reformation had had little impact on Norwegian Catholicism.

The Archbishop at Nidaros, an outspoken advocate of Norwegian independence, was forced to flee. Powerful monasteries and convents were dissolved and their significant real-estate holdings seized. At the same time prominent government positions and estates in Norway were transferred to Danish nobility, and many Norwegian place names were respelled or changed to Danish. The medieval city of Oslo burned in 1624 and was rebuilt in another nearby location that was protected by the Akershus fortress. Danish King Christian IV gave it the new name "Christiania" and administration of Norway was centered there for the rulers in Copenhagen.[5]

SWEDISH RULE

The Kalmar Union between Norway and Denmark ended officially after the defeat of French Emperor Napoleon Bonaparte in 1814. Denmark had backed Napoleon, and the victorious allies included Sweden, to which Norway was given as one of the spoils of war. The terms of the settlement actually appeared favorable to Norway which, although linked to Sweden, would be termed independent, self-governing and self-taxing. Despite that, Christian Frederik, the Danish-born governor of Norway and nephew of the Danish king, successfully stirred Norwegian nationalism, leading to a rejection of the Swedish alliance.

A Norwegian assembly at Eidsvold adopted a national constitution on May 17, 1814, and elected Frederik King of Norway. The date, *Syttende Mai*, became an enduring national day of celebration for all Norwegians. Sweden, however, would not surrender its claim, and sent its military to enforce jurisdiction over poorly-armed and under-fortified Norway.

Christian Frederik was compelled to end his very short-term reign after only three months. The Swedes accepted the Eidsvold Constitution but with amendments pertaining to a union of the two countries; the two realms were to have one king and stand together in war, but in all other respects be independent of each other and on an equal footing.

Swedish King Charles XIII, with the oversight of Sweden's parliament, began his rule over Norway from the Royal Court in Stockholm. Construction began on a palace in Christiania which would serve as the official residence of members of the Royal Family while in Norway. In 1877 the name of the capital was changed from the Danish "Christiania" to the more Nordic "Kristiania."

The reign of King Oscar II (1829-1907) and Queen Sofie (1836-1913), the last Swedish rulers of Norway, was a difficult period between Norway and Sweden, ending with the dissolution of their union in 1905.

During the ninety-one years that followed the writing of the constitution, although under the rule of five Swedish kings, Norway was able to build its marketing, manufacturing and shipping sectors, but was frustrated by the prohibition against establishing an independent foreign consular service in order to make direct foreign commercial and diplomatic connections. Swedish kings repeatedly resisted petitions for that right, and Norway prepared for a break by strengthening fortifications along the mutual border and enlarging its army and navy.

Finally, in 1905 the Norwegian cabinet of Swedish King Oscar II resigned, leaving him without constitutional authority to rule Norway. He had been deposed on a technicality, but this time Sweden chose not to threaten military force in response to the provocation. The union of 1814 dissolved peacefully and Norway was recognized as an independent state by Sweden and all other countries. The first country to formally recognize Norway's independence was the United States of America.

THE MODERN NORWEGIAN MONARCHY

In 1905 the Eidsvold Constitution was in place, and had been for 91 years, but a choice remained for the transitional leaders of the newly-independent government: a constitutional monarchy or a republic. Four hundred years under foreign monarchs had left good memories and bad, and Norwegians weighed their seemingly conflicting desires to celebrate the Norwegian traditions or to become a thoroughly modern, progressive country. Those favoring monarchy surveyed those European royals with the highest probability of Norwegian ancestry, and then secretly made contact with 33 year-old Prince Christian Frederik Carl Georg Valdemar Axel, the second son of King Frederik VIII of Denmark.

Prince Carl's mother, Queen Louise, was the daughter of King Charles XV of Sweden. Carl was married to Princess Maud, youngest daughter of British King Edward VII and Queen Alexandra, daughter of King Kristian IX of Denmark. The newly-independent

Norway was eager for alliances, so Prince Carl's marital ties to England were attractive. The fact that Carl and Maud had a two-year-old son, Prince Alexander Edward Christian Frederik, automatically prevented a future succession headache.

Article six of the Norwegian Constitution of 1814 and 1905 specified *Agnatic Primogeniture*: male-only succession to the throne as drawn from early sixth-century German *Salic* law. The first-born surviving son of a king was the called crown prince and was destined to succeed his father as king. Daughters were not eligible. At that time an alternate practice called *Cognatic Primogeniture* was used by the predominately rural common Norwegian population. Commonly called *odelsrett* for "rights of the oldest", under it the oldest male was again the primary beneficiary, but in the absence of sons an oldest daughter could inherit the family estate. This practice ensured that farms and businesses remained intact and viable for taxation, rather than being subdivided toward insignificance with the passing of each generation. A daughter beneficiary was expected to find a husband to operate the farm or business.

KING HAAKON VII AND QUEEN MAUD

Count Fritz Wedel Jarlsberg, who would later become the recipient of the Nobel Peace Prize, and distinguished Norwegian polar explorer Fridtjof Nansen negotiated an agreement with the prospective king, to establish a constitutional monarchy in Norway. Prince Carl recognized that there were conflicting opinions on the need for a monarchy in Norway, so before accepting the crown he insisted that the issue be put before the people. The plebiscite, which was one of the first to include women, yielded an almost eighty percent majority in favor of the monarchy. The *Storting* (Norwegian Parliament) unanimously elected Prince Carl to be the first of the new line of hereditary kings of Norway. To demonstrate the sincerity of his motto: *Alt for Norge* (All for Norway), Carl dropped the use of his numerous traditional family names and chose to become Haakon VII, linking himself to Viking kings. In the same spirit, Haakon changed his son's name to Olav.

On June 22, 1906 King Haakon VII and Queen Maud were crowned at Nidaros Cathedral in Trondheim in accordance with the 1814 Constitution. That constitution had granted the king executive powers, but in the 1905 parliamentary constitutional monarchy it was clear that the duties of a king would be limited to representing Norway at civic and foreign events. A king and crown prince, when of age, would also preside over the Council of State. That body included the prime minister and other select government officials and it exercised duties in the name of the king. The council began to meet at the Royal Palace in

After the dissolution of the union with Sweden in 1905, Prince Carl of Denmark (1872-1957) was chosen King of Norway, taking the name of Haakon; Princess Maud of Great Britain (1869-1938) became the Queen.

15

Kristiania on a regular basis. That palace, though built by the Swedish monarchy, became the home of the Norwegian Royal Family and has retained ceremonial and administrative functions since 1905.

From the first days of the reign of Haakon VII, some Norwegians complained about the potential costs of maintaining the Royal Family. King Haakon watched royal expenses closely and became trusted by even his harshest critics. Over the years the Royal Family has had various estates available as private dwellings. Some of these were owned by the state, others were gifts to the monarchy, and a few were royal purchases.[6]

CROWN PRINCE OLAV

Crown Prince Olav was born (as Prince Alexander) July 2, 1903 in the United Kingdom. His earliest environment and training were English, and to some extent that orientation continued after his move to Norway. Queen Maud was an English woman and never attained fluency in the Norwegian language. She regularly attended the Anglican Church, St. Edmund's, in central Kristiania/Oslo, sometimes with King Haakon.[7]

As a result of her difficulty with the language and affinity to the Anglican church, Queen Maud was, perhaps unfairly, characterized as aloof by those members of the press and public prone to criticize the monarchy. To accommodate her, household members and staff needed to be bilingual.

Maud brought Prince Olav's British nanny, Miss Annie Butler, along on the move to Norway. Miss Butler continued to tutor the Crown Prince, but Norwegian teachers worked with her to give Olav language skills to enable him to keep pace with his school contemporaries. His Norwegian assimilation also included training in sailing, a sport that he pursued enthusiastically for the remainder of his life. In the 1928 Olympics he earned Norway a gold medal in the six-meter sailboat competition. He also excelled in Nordic and Alpine skiing, and he ski-jumped at the renowned *Holmenkollen* national facility near the Royal Mountain Farm, *Kongsseteren*.

The education of the Crown Prince was planned to prepare him for his future role as the titular head of the armed forces. Prince Olav graduated from the Norwegian Military Academy in 1924. After leaving the military academy, Olav studied jurisprudence and economics at Balliol Collage in Oxford, England. His skills later proved valuable to Norway and the Allies during and after World War II.[8]

King Olav (1903-1991) succeeded his father to the throne of Norway in 1957; Princess Märtha (1901-1954) of Sweden became his wife in 1929.

PRINCE HARALD IS BORN TO CROWN PRINCESS MÄRTHA AND CROWN PRINCE OLAV

On March 21, 1929 Crown Prince Olav married Märtha Sofia Lovisa Dagmar Thyra, Princess of Sweden. She was the daughter of Prince Charles of Sweden and Princess Ingeborg of Denmark, and therefore a cousin to Olav. Ironically, she had been a Princess of Norway and Sweden from her birth in 1901 until the 1905 separation of the two countries.

Theirs was the first royal wedding in Norway in 554 years. As a wedding gift Minister (Herman) Fritz Wedel Jarlsberg presented to the new Royal Couple the Skaugum estate in the town of Asker. The property was located in a then-rural setting overlooking the Oslofjord, 15 miles southwest of Oslo.

The Crown Prince and Crown Princess moved into their new home soon after the wedding. The next year they were expecting the birth of their first child, when on May 20, Skaugum burned to the ground. Princess Ragnhild was born twenty days later on June 9, 1930. Architect Arnstein Arneberg was commissioned to create a modern, comfortable and functional replacement home, more for family living than state receptions. The new Skaugum building was completed in 1932.

The second daughter, Princess Astrid, was born on February 12th of that year, but the country awaited a male to be heir to the throne. On February 21, 1937 Prince Harald was born.[9]

CROWNS AND SCEPTERS SEPARATED THE ROYALS FROM THE PEOPLE

Over the centuries, there was always a gulf between the royalty that ruled a country and their subjects. This style of leadership changed dramatically in Norway during the twentieth century. The three royal wedding photos on these pages show clearly the transition from the formal coronation with royal crowns and scepters of King Haakon and Queen Maud in 1905 to the later informal consecration of Crown Prince Olav and Crown Princess Märtha, and Crown Prince Harald and Crown Princess Sonja. Thus, today the Royal family is known to be approachable by the Norwegian people.

King Harold with Haakon Magnus holding the future Queen of Norway, Ingrid Alexandra.
In the background, King Olav, King Haakon and Crown Princess Märtha.

King Harald V (b. 1937) came to the throne in 1991; his wife, Queen Sonja (b. 1937) was the first Norwegian-born Queen since the Middle Ages.

Inga Berg's Family History and Early Life

High above the Begna River, the Reinli *Stavkirke* (ca. 1250) was the third church in succession to have risen on its mountaintop site. Long before it a *Heithinh hof* (Old Norse temple) was burned there during the eleventh century Christianization of the Valdres province.

In the valley below, the village of Bagn was surrounded by a cluster of centuries-old farms. The farms took many of their names from the terrain, and the Norwegians took their

names from the farms on which they worked. Most farms were divided into sub-farms and those were divided into smaller plots, some with cottages for the tenant-worker families. Those families were large, and the scant amounts of arable land could not support further division. Division rarely occurred anyway because the traditional inheritance practice was *odelsrett* (rights of the oldest). If land were owned, the oldest male son inherited all. If there were no sons, the oldest daughter was the sole beneficiary and a very desirable bride. Younger sons who wished to farm could

The *Reinli Stavkirke* (1250 – The Reinli Stave Church), as it appeared in 1903, is one of the best preserved of the 29 stave churches still standing in Norway.

become tenant farmers. Successive European economic depressions compounded problems, causing Valdres to lead all regions of Norway in nineteenth century per-capita emigration to the United States.[10]

MARTIN OLSEN AND MARIT OLSDOTTER

June 23, 1890 Martin Olsen, 31, married 24-year-old Marit Olsdotter Arneson Ellendshaugen who was a beneficiary of her father's estate. (Martin and his family later took the surname

Berg, from the name of the farm that they acquired. Tenant farmers, called *husmenn,* took their surnames from the name of the land they worked and when they moved, their names and their children's last names changed too.) Martin came from a poor family in Dølvesknatten, and probably had been working for a time as a laborer and carpenter at farms around Bagn. His bride, however, was the daughter of a prosperous local farmer named Ola Ellendshaugen. Perhaps Martin's advantages over other suitors had been his ambition and aptitude to adopt a trade and to eventually raise his family above the *bruker* tenant farmer class.

The newlyweds did begin as *brukere* on a leased plot of land on the large Erstad Farm. Their plot was on the

Photographs of Marit and Martin Berg, parents of Inga Berg, are framed in a locket taken to America by her sister, Marie.

west side of the Begna River on a sub-farm named *Liffengren*, (probably a proper name). Martin was under contract as a *husmann* who with his family was entitled to occupy, but not own a cottage and plot, in exchange for part-time labor. Their farmer-landlord, Hans Erikson Thorsrud, had a sideline as a *hjulmaker* (wheelwright), and Martin satisfied part of his work obligation by assisting him in that business. The arrangement enabled Martin to hone generally useful woodworking and blacksmithing skills that were required in the *hjulmaker* trade.[11]

GROWING A FAMILY

Marie Martinsdotter Liffengren Olsen, the first child of Martin and Marit, was born in September of 1891. By tradition her given name and that of each of her future siblings, was followed by a derivation of her father's given name, and by the name of the farm where her family lived. Martin chose to have his children also retain his family name "Olsen" while they resided on leased property. ("Olsen" with an "e" is a Danish variation, while "Olson" is Swedish. Norway's years under changing foreign dominion caused both versions to be in common usage.)

The names of the subsequent children did not include *Liffengren* because the family moved in 1892 to an adjacent farm called *Øvervøll* (lit. upper embankment). Over the next six years, with financial assistance from the new landlord Amund Amundson Vøll, Martin built a wooden frame house and small outbuildings on the leased plot. Martin was also hired out for other local carpentry work, and continued to apprentice with wheelwright Thorsrud.

Thea Martinsdotter Øvervøll Olsen was born in December of 1892, and the first boy, Ola (born as Ole but changed the name later to Ola) Martinson Øvervøll Olsen, followed in August of 1894. As the first male, Ola would be the heir to the family property.

Inga Martinsdotter Øvervøll Olsen, born February 7, 1896, was the third and last girl. The next year the Olsen family moved again, this time to land that they leased from Marit's father, located just off the Bagn town square. Ola Ellendshaugen also owned sub-farms called *Bergene* (on the hillside) and *Bagn Øvre* (Bagn farm higher up).

The family of Martin and Marit had a new name, *Berg* (mountain), (*Bergene* is the plural form of Berg). Berg was the name that all of the family members would keep despite some future individual relocations.

The family occupied a small building named *Brustugu* (bridge house), near the bridge that crossed the Begna River at the *Storefoss* (large falls). Just below the bridge house was a sawmill powered by the falls, above was the Fjellheim Hotel, and across the square a dairy cooperative. The cluster of buildings was known as *Storebrofossen Plassen* (large falls bridge square). In 1915 other stores were opened including a goldsmith, shoemaker, a drying shed and Martin's wheelwright shop.

Inga Berg's name appears sixth from the top in the Berg family Bible on the page titled *Bogen Tilhörer* (lit. this book belongs to; the title was intended to mean family tree).

19

Martin helped his father-in-law work the *Bergene* farm and along with Marit grew food crops on the family plot. They also raised goats, pigs and cows. In his precious spare time Martin began to build from the ground up a more substantial multi-use structure to replace *Brustugu*. When the stone foundation of the basement level of the new building was complete it was put to immediate use, divided between a barn and a wheelwright shop. The family continued to grow as two more boys, Oddmund in 1897 and Arne in 1899, were born. The last two sons, Gunnar and Magne, were born in 1904 and 1907.

NORWEGIAN SCHOOLS

A Norwegian law from 1848 stipulated that every town would maintain a permanent school with compulsory attendance for children from the age of seven. The two-storied log *Øystre Bagn* School (on the east side of river) that Inga and her siblings attended was located across the road from the Bagn Parish Church, about a half mile from Bridge Square.

Bas-relief of the highly respected Ole Thorsrud who was the teacher of the Berg family children and was *klokker* (song leader) who led congregational singing at the Bagn church.

In the school, emphasis was placed on reading, writing, mathematics, and studying from books on science, history and geography. Courses like needlework developed practical skills, while such subjects as art, singing and "song theory" gave the children a well-rounded education.

Schoolmaster Ole Thorsrud was also the church choir director. He stressed the study of religion because it was a required subject. A goal of education and of the Norwegian Lutheran State Church was to have students progress toward confirmation by learning to read and comprehend the Holy Scriptures as interpreted by Martin Luther. Young Norwegians were confirmed at about the same age that they finished grammar school. They were then considered to be adults proven capable of conducting a principled life and ready to take on greater responsibility. A diploma and a certificate of good character from the minister were both important references for employment.[12]

At the end of their last year children in school were graded on all of their subjects. Each student was also separately evaluated for continuing education. The expectation, however, that young women should continue study in a vocational specialty was almost nil. Adult male role models were professionals like their male teachers. The only female role models for the Berg sisters were homemakers like their mother, cousins and aunts, none of whom had gone beyond the elementary education offered in Bagn.

Although Marie and Thea received excellent marks and excellent evaluations, neither projected herself in a professional role and neither pursued additional education. They did prepare themselves for pre-marriage employment, but in typical women's specialties complementary to domestic service and homemaking. Thea became adept at needlework and sewing, and Marie at ironing. The latter was a difficult task, prone to specialization in the pre-electric steam iron times when iron temperature controls were particularly challenging.

At the beginning of the Twentieth Century, Norway was poised to permanently end centuries of foreign dominion. Events of national and of Berg family significance transpired in succession. On July 2, 1903 Inga Berg's future employer, Danish Prince Alexander, was born to Prince Carl and Princess Maud. One year later Inga's fourth brother, Gunner Martinson Berg, was born. Two more years passed during which Norway gained independence from Sweden, Prince Carl was crowned as King Haakon VII of Norway, and his toddler son Prince Alexander of Denmark became Crown Prince Olav of Norway.

TRAGEDY CHANGES THE FAMILY LIFE

In the late 1800s nearly every Norwegian birth still occurred in the home and was assisted by a *jordmor* (midwife) rather than the community doctor. It was a centuries-old practice but over the previous hundred years the quality of midwifery in Norway had been greatly improved. Lay midwives had been replaced by professionally trained and certified public servants, but they were still limited in expertise and by the home setting. In those circumstances there were few options for easing certain complicated deliveries. The nearest hospital to Bagn could be reached only after many miles of travel over rough roads in a horse-drawn buggy. On August 25, 1907 Marit Berg had her eighth child, a fifth son who was named Magne, but the birth did not go well. The trauma of a breech delivery took the life of the 42-year-old mother, and left her newborn child mentally impaired. This was a staggering blow to Martin Berg who was left alone to provide for a large

Inga Berg, far left, was pictured at the age of 11 in 1907 at the time of the death of her mother, Marit Oldsdotter Ellendshaugen Berg. Other members of the family from left to right were: Martin (father), Oddmund, Ola, Thea, Marie and in the front row, Gunnar and Arne.

family, but he drew consolation from the fact that he had three daughters, two of whom had reached the accepted age of responsibility.

NEW RESPONSIBILITIES FOR THE CHILDREN

Each child in the Berg family, by the time he or she reached eight years of age, had been assigned chores around the wheel shop, garden and house. Girls were supposed to help their mother do all the work around the home while the boys assisted the father with farming, carpentry and wheel-making.

When Marit died, Marie and Thea (nearly16 and 14) had completed their required schooling. They, and to a lesser degree 11-year-old Inga, were now expected to also fill their mother's role in cooking, cleaning and producing clothing for the rest of the family.

At first women from the neighborhood and extended family came in to assist with the newborn child, but eventually the sisters alone were meeting almost all of Magne's needs. It was a daunting situation for all of the children, and father Martin was a stern taskmaster.

The Berg sisters made clothing from sturdy wool or linen fabrics. The materials were spun, woven and dyed at home. In the outside laundry shed they scrubbed diapers on a washboard in a tub, and boiled white linens over a small wood-burning stove. They served four meals each day: *frokost* (lit. early food) was the first breakfast and consisted of coffee and *flatbrød* (flat bread) or *hardangerlefse*. *Dugurd* (the meal eaten in late morning) included *grøt* with cheese or jam. In Norway *grøt* is a soft food made of cereal or meal boiled in water or milk until thick. This is not as thick as American oatmeal because oats are too hard to break down to be soft enough for babies. On Sundays and other special days the girls might have also served meat and boiled potatoes. The third meal, *nonslid,* was served around three o'clock in the afternoon. It was similar to farmers' afternoon coffee, and featured open face sandwiches. At around seven o'clock the sisters served the last meal of the day *kvelds* (supper), which consisted of *grøt a*nd sour milk.

OWNING PROPERTY

After Marit's death, her father sold the Bridge Square property to Martin for a modest price and also donated some money and materials for completion of the family home. Martin and his older sons assisted hired workers with the final construction. The Bergs moved out of *Brustugu* and that building was later demolished. At Bridge Square Martin and sons eventually built two other buildings that would serve the Berg family and the community, *Fjellvik* (bay where the ground is rocky) and *Midtberg* (middle hill). Martin continued to run the wheelwright business in the lower level walkout of the large building and the family filled the living space on the two and one-half floors above. The home was large but simply furnished. Heat was drawn from wood-burning stoves, one of which was also used for cooking. Candles and oil lamps provided light. The children shared four bedrooms on the second floor.

SOME BERG CHILDREN LEAVE HOME

Martin was known to be not only demanding but also quite frugal, or *gjerrig* (stingy) as some locals from Bagn would say. Those characteristics in their father, as well as the heavy workload weighed on the Berg sisters. The three were tied down by family chores with little free time to socialize except when going to church or when participating in the Women's Temperance Union. The lack of career opportunities and of suitors who would own property in rural Norway made their futures in Bagn quite bleak. Over the next several tedious years each girl weighed options and developed a course of action.

When Marie was around 18 years old, she made her first move toward independence by taking on some outside work for spending money. One of her jobs may have been as a housekeeper at the Fjellheim Hotel or for wealthy families in the Bagn area. Thea also began to do odd jobs outside of the family home. Of course, this left Inga with a greater share of household tasks.

A statue of Dr. Hallgrim Evjen, the village doctor whose office and home was next door to the Bergs. He had a considerable influence on Inga's choice of profession.

The Bergs corresponded with relatives who, after emigrating, were touting the opportunities in *Amerika*. By 1912 Marie had decided to emigrate, and Thea accompanied her. Older cousin Arne Bang and his wife Nellie in Granite Falls, Minnesota helped them purchase steamship tickets, agreeing that after arrival the two young women would stay for the first summer at the Bang farm to help with both housekeeping and the care of their two children. Martin constructed one small wooden trunk in which the two sisters were able to carry only a few of their possessions to begin their new lives.

Marie and Thea left from Kristiania for England on April 17, 1912. Their April 29 scheduled departure from Southampton on the White Star liner *Olympic* was cancelled when that ship was pressed into North Atlantic service after the loss of its sister ship *Titanic*. Marie and Thea finally sailed from Liverpool on May 2 aboard the White Star's *Cedric* and arrived at Ellis Island in New York on May 12. They took five more days to travel to Granite Falls, Minnesota; the entire journey lasted almost a month.[13]

The White Star ship, *Olympic*, is shown on this postcard which her sister Marie sent to Inga on April 29, 1912. The photograph below is of the *Cedric*, the ship they finally took from Liverpool on May 2, 1912.

Sixteen-year-old Inga was the only young woman left to manage the Berg household. She remained there for five more years. During that time she followed by mail the American assimilation of her sisters in Minnesota, but began preparing herself for an entirely different way of life.

Inga's Training and Education

In April of 1912, when Marie and Thea Berg left Bagn, Norway for new lives in America, sixteen-year-old Inga was better prepared to assume the woman's responsibilities in the Berg household than her sisters had been after their mother's sudden death five years earlier. Inga was the only female left at home but the family was smaller by two; the remaining boys had grown to greater maturity. Although Magne had become a strong and very active five-year-old whose mental disability compounded the difficulty in his handling, Inga had the help of five males to channel his energy. She also had a knack for organizing and for managing herself and others.

PRIMARY AND SECONDARY EDUCATION

Inga, like her sisters before her, finished primary school with good marks and a favorable assessment for continuing education, but she had the exceptional element in her character that drove her to be one of the rare women of the time to actually pursue a professional career.

Marie and Thea informally acquired specialties that were within the traditional in-home woman's role of the time. Realistically, outside jobs in ironing or needlework were unlikely to be more than stopgaps until the sisters found husband-breadwinners. Inga, however, chose the infant care field with a specific goal to work for others. She probably received her secondary education at the *framhaldsskole* (South Aurdal Continuing Education School), a one-year non-vocational program following grammar school, and also found work assisting local midwives. In 1920, at the age of 24, Inga enrolled in a one-year course of instruction at the *Jordmorskolen* (Midwives School) at the *Kvinneklinikken* (Women's Clinic), a part of the *Rikshospitalet* (State Hospital) in Christiania.

In all forms of early medicine, transportation issues caused large parts of northern European countries to lag behind the rest of Europe in innovation, structure and standardization. Right into the 20th century, landmarks of medicine for Norway came first to the larger population centers of Oslo and Bergen but, due to the small numbers of professionals to administer them, were especially slow to reach rural areas.

TRAINING AS MIDWIFE

Midwifery (attending to a woman in childbirth) is one of the world's earliest occupations, recognized in the Old Testament and in writings from ancient Greece and Rome. *Jordmor*, the Norwegian word for midwife, translates literally as "earth mother." For centuries it was a lay practice with passed-down procedures performed by women of the community. In the early formalization of the medical profession in seventeenth century Denmark-Norway,

A sketch of a midwife's uniform from the 1920s, taken from the 175th Yearbook of the Midwife School in Oslo.

midwives were placed for the first time under the authority of doctors. There were very few doctors. In 1740 doctor accreditation began with the opening of a state medical school in Copenhagen, and training programs for midwives followed. By 1810 midwife accreditation had also begun and a statewide network of publicly-paid and certified midwives was established. There were still only about 54 certified midwives in Norway shortly before the 1814 split with Denmark. Norway addressed the problem by founding its own institutions, starting with the *Rikshospitalet* in Christiania. In 1818 the *Jordmorskolen* was established. That school was ninety-nine years old when Inga enrolled in the two-year program[14] and by this time it had graduated over 2,700 students. Even now midwives remain important. In the year 2005 over 2,000 midwives were practicing in Norway.

Inga received one of the top overall grades in her class at the *Jordmorskolen*, in both the written and practical examinations. After she completed studies in 1922, *Søster* Annie Krogh Koren, the school director, gave her excellent recommendations and contacts within the wealthier families of Oslo. Inga began delivering babies with the well-established midwife Anna Thomassen and, as she gained experience and exposure, Inga attracted her own clientele.[15]

Inga's first long-term infant nursing position was with the Klara (*née* Overbye) and Kristian Bleka family. She knew the family in Bagn so this arrangement was a comfortable first experience. The Blekas had moved to Oslo in 1890 and built a three story, ten-unit apartment house on Pro.f Dahls Gate 19. Inga had a private room on the first floor overlooking a flowered courtyard.

Inga was very entrepreneurial in finding families; she opted to live in the homes of wealthy families for up to six to eight months and sometimes longer as in the case of the Royal Family. With few resources and the low salaries of nurses in general, these arrangements meant that she did not have to keep an expensive apartment in Oslo.

She decided instead to rent a room in a boarding house for church workers from Fr. Serine Muus at Nils Juels Gate 66b in Hersted located in central Oslo. Because of her close connection to the Lutheran church, Inga fit right into the house life and made many friends whom she called *damene våre* (our ladies). She lived here between contracts and when not in her *Midtberg* home in Bagn.

PEDIATRIC NURSE TRAINING IN LONDON

Twentieth century advances in obstetrics and gynecology would eventually cause a shift in child delivery locations from homes to hospitals. The role of midwives would also broaden to include counseling on family planning services and on pre- and post-natal care. Those changes would make safe and efficient birthing available to Norwegians of all economic

classes, but Inga's well-to-do client base in 1920s-Oslo expected traditional home service from the best private midwives available. Inga was usually called to spend about two weeks in residence at a home and then would move on to another. Although she had become a successful midwife, Inga disliked the unstable routine, and noticed that pediatric nurses typically spent one to two years in home residence after a birth. That was one reason why she decided to broaden her childcare expertise. At that time the pediatric nurse

Inga Berg, top left, holding a newborn baby was photographed in Oslo at the *Kvinneklinikken* (Woman's Clinic) along with other nurses at the bedside of a mother who had just delivered quintuplets.

education program in Norway was not well developed. *Søster* Koren of the *Jordmorskolen* encouraged Inga's new career goal and advised her to go to England in order to receive the best training.[16]

St. Thomas' Hospital was first built in the twelfth century and was dedicated to Thomas à Becket. Two of the associated hospitals later established to meet specific needs were Guy's Hospital and Evelina Children's Hospital. The former was founded by Sir Thomas Guy and opened in 1776 in order to treat the "incurable" who had been denied admission to St. Thomas. Baron Ferdinand Rothschild financed the building of Evelina Children's Hospital in memory of his wife who, like Marit Berg, had died in childbirth. It opened in 1869 and treatment began for infant children who at the time were succumbing in astonishing numbers to infectious diseases, tuberculosis, and nerve and lung disorders.

In Norway and in the rest of Europe formal training and certification came later for nursing than for midwifery. During the 1850s Crimean War, Englishwoman Florence Nightingale and her team of nurses earned acclaim by organizing field hospitals and identifying sources of contamination. Nightingale brought attention to the value of nursing as a profession and also wrote the definitive nurses' textbook, *Notes on Nursing: What It Is, and What It Is Not.*[17] She channeled donations into the 1860 founding of the Nightingale Training School and Home for Nurses at St. Thomas Hospital, London. It was the world's first professional nurses school. Nurses trained at the Nightingale School and the Mother Institut at Kaisersworth, Germany came to Norway and founded nursing programs in small nursing homes and later at the State Hospital (*Rikshospitalet*) and others, and in 1915 formed a nurses' association *Sykepleierforbundet* (sick nursing organization). In Norway, sick nurses dealt with ill patients; other nurses could care for children or others who are not ill.)[18]

Around 1924 Inga traveled to London and used her solid references as a student of Annie Krogh Koren, Director of the midwife program at the women's clinic, and Anna Thomassen, a practicing midwife in Oslo, to secure employment with prominent British pediatrician and medical researcher, Dr. E. I. Lloyd. Dr. Lloyd was also an instructor at the Nightingale School. By working and studying under him Inga was able to combine the best academic and vocational pediatric training of the time, and also to polish her fluency in English.

PROFESSIONAL NURSING PRACTICE

Inga returned to Norway in 1927 with burnished credentials and references. Anna Thomassen referred Inga to clients of increasingly high social status, including Lilanne and Maximillian ("Max") Carden Despard. Despard was a British navy officer, later to become a naval *attaché*

Inga is shown holding baby Anita Maud Despard, child of one of the key families to support her application for a position at Skaugum.

in Oslo, and his wife [*née* Hurum] was a Norwegian. The couple had met at a dance and reception at the Royal Palace in 1923 where Queen Maud introduced them. Their child, Anita Maud Despard, was born in 1927. The Queen was a namesake and a godmother with a significant interest in the child's welfare. Inga was chosen by the Despards as midwife to deliver the baby, and then serve as pediatric nurse-in-residence. Queen Maud first witnessed Inga's professional technique on a visit to the Despard home.[19]

After leaving the Despards, Inga worked for ten years in the homes of many other well-established families in the Oslo area including industrialist Alf Tjersland and his wife Thora. The Tjerslands recommended Inga's services to the Royal Family at an opportune time because Crown Princess Märtha was pregnant with her third child. In January of 1937 Inga was interviewed at the Royal Palace in Oslo and was immediately hired to be the pediatric nurse for the expected prince or princess. On February 21 the future king of Norway, Prince Harald, was born with Annie Krogh Koren, Director of the Jordmorskolen, presiding as midwife and Prof. Dr. Anton Sunde as attending obstetrician. Seventeen days later on March 10 Inga Berg began her service as Prince Harald's nurse.

Throughout her training and her career in Oslo, Inga stayed close to her family and to Bagn, her hometown. Some of her Berg siblings followed a pattern familiar to Norwegians: two younger brothers Arne and Gunnar emigrated to America in 1922 and 1924 respectively. When Martin Berg died in 1925, the Berg property went to oldest son Ola. He and his wife, Inga Olsdotter Brendingen, opened a tailor shop in the big house and lived above. The Fjellvik building was subdivided from the other Berg properties and Oddmund bought it from Ola in 1925, the year their father died. He opened a cabinet shop in one part of the building, and his wife, Netta Johannesdotter Engen, opened a café in another. The two later moved to Hønefoss where Oddmund opened a window and sash company. The Midtberg house, which had been leased as a post office in 1920, was also subdivided, and in 1927 Inga and her brother Gunnar bought it from Ola. In 1933 Gunnar sold his share of the Midtberg house to Inga.

Inga's Life at Skaugum

For 18 months Inga Berg noted in her journal the physical and behavioral development of Prince Harald. The task chart (Appendix Five) indicates that she had an all-consuming job with enormous responsibility. Inga wrote of many duties she had not expected before she began her employment. She kept detailed records of the Prince's milk intake, also recording other foods he ate, and charted his weight. She wrote about his relationships with family members, the appearance of his first tooth, and other details, general and minute, of his daily life. She listed in her journal the visitors to Skaugum and people she met on trips abroad. Inga tucked into her journal the photos she had taken of Prince Harald, along with newspaper clippings and official photographs of the infant prince.[20]

ACCOMMODATIONS AT SKAUGUM

The Skaugum estate stands 600 feet above sea level and offers magnificent views of the Oslo Fjord. The main building is surrounded by thirty-eight acres of elaborate gardens, 120 acres of farmland and facilities and 125 acres of forest. During her service Inga's private room was next to Prince Harald's nursery on the second floor. The first floor was furnished for family living, although there were also eight elegant rooms for entertaining and four staff rooms for the chef, servants and guards.[21]

THE STAFF

In 1937-38 the Skaugum staff primarily assisted Crown Prince Olav and Crown Princess Märtha in the planning and execution of their various official duties. About 20 people— butlers, chef, cooks, housekeepers, nurses, tutors and gardeners—kept Skaugum in operation. Additional staff tended the Skaugum farm. A manager and three permanent assistants maintained buildings and operated equipment for agriculture and forestry. The main farm products produced were grain, milk and meat. The livestock included about one hundred head of cattle.

In 1937 the Crown Prince's Equerry was Colonel Nikolai Østgaard. [Equerry is a British military term for a personal attendant to a royal family.] Colonel Østgaard functioned like a managing director of a company. He worked with two assistants, one for Crown Prince Olav, and another for Crown Princess Märtha. Additional staff included two ladies-in-waiting and three assistant equerries. These latter positions were honorary and changed every month according to a set schedule. An equerry and lady-in-waiting accompanied the Crown Prince and Crown Princess on official engagements, always a few steps behind but nearby in case they were needed.

Prince Harald in his baby carriage, was pictured with the Skaugum staff. Seated on the left was the head chef and next to her was Crown Princess Märtha's personal assistant; standing, was Inga Berg and in front of her were some other staff members.

Each week Colonel Østgaard and his two assistants met with the Royal Couple to plan activities for the week and for the future. Careful planning ensured that activities proceeded without mistakes. Crown Prince Olav and Crown Princess Märtha made all the final decisions, but they left the details to the staff. The staff collaborated with local officials on planning trips within Norway, but trips abroad were usually handled by the Department of Foreign Affairs. The Skaugum staff managed all correspondence and invitations to events. Requests from citizens were referred to other appropriate departments or institutions. Fan mail, especially to the children, was answered, and usually pictures were included.[22]

Prince Harald grew up at Skaugum in Asker, twelve miles southwest of Oslo on the Oslofjorden.

Floor Plan of Skaugum

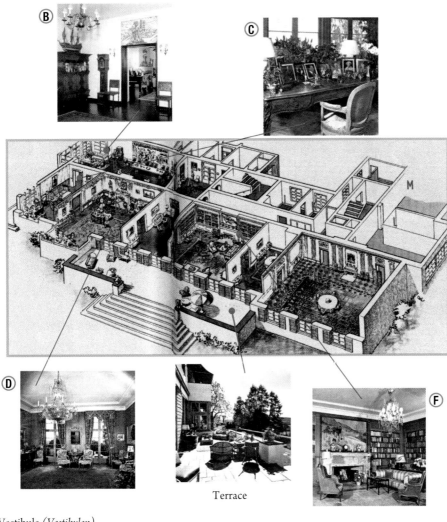

Terrace

A   Vestibule (*Vestibylen*)
B   Great Room (*Hallen*)
C   Smoking Room (*Røkeværelset*)
D   Crown Princesses' Drawing Room (*Kronprinsessens Salong*)
E   Garden Room (*Hagestuen*)
F   Library (*Biblioteket*)
G   Breakfast Room (*Frokostværelset*)
H   Dining Room (*Spisesalen*)
I   Main stairway from 1st and 2nd floor (*Hovedtrapp mellom 1. og 2. Etasje*)
J   Office for Aide-de-camp (*Kontor for Adjutanter*)
K   Guard Room (*Vaktrom*)
L   Chef and Butler Area (*Kjøkken og anretning*)
M   Servants' Quarters (*Tjenerfløyen*)

Note: the nursery, laundry, and children's rooms are on the second floor and east wing, and are not shown here.

ROYAL PALACE

Inga often traveled outside Skaugum with Prince Harald and the Royal Family. The Royal Palace in Oslo, considered the King's official residence, was mentioned many times in Inga's journal. For Norwegians the palace was and is a focal point and symbol of the modern monarchy as well as a tie to old traditions.

Akershus Castle, built around 1300, served as a formal palace in medieval times, but by the time of the Sweden-Norway alliance of 1814 it no longer fit the modern European model for a palace. Swedish-Norwegian King Charles III (Karl Johan) ordered the construction of a new palace in the center of Christiania as his Norwegian residence, but did not live to see it completed.

The Royal Palace is located in the center of Oslo on a small hill. It dominates the city and is a link between Norway's past and her present.

Built between 1825 and 1849, the flat-roofed, three-story brick building was the largest and most expensive building attempted in Norway since the thirteenth-century Nidaros Cathedral in Trondheim.

During the union with Sweden, Kings Oscar I, Charles IV and Oscar II, used the Palace on their visits to Christiania. In 1905 it became a permanent residence for the new Royal Family of Norway, King Haakon VII, Queen Maud and their three-year-old son, Prince Olav.

The Royal Palace served many functions. On the first floor were grand reception rooms and a chapel, banquet hall, ballroom and private dining room. The King and Queen had a private apartment and offices in the Palace. The Crown Prince and Princess also had offices there but lived at Skaugum. Every Friday the Council of State met at the Palace. The Council included leaders of government and the *Storting*, plus the King and Crown Prince. Other uses of the Palace included formal and informal audiences, annual dinners for government officials and banquets for visiting foreign heads of state.[23]

In addition to the Royal Palace and Skaugum, the Royal Family at different times owned or had use of seven other residences. Four were near Oslo: the Royal Farm at *Bygdøy*, the *Kongsseteren* (Royal Mountain Farm), *Bloksberg* (Island cabin), and a vacation residence on Mågerø Island. The summer house (*hytte*) on this island is rather new to the family properties. The family of Sonja, Harald's future wife, had a summer house on nearby Tjøme Island that Harald and Sonja used the first years they were married. They later built a summer house on Måterø which was finished in 1998. This area is military land and secluded from the public. Three others are *Gamlehaugen* in Bergen, *Stiftsgården* in Trondheim and *Ledaal* in Stavanger.

PART II

Text and Translation of Prins Harald's Dagbook

—written by Inga Berg

Inga ordered a red, leather-bound book with gold leaf lettering for her journal.

Introduction

The historical information in the previous section provides context for an intensive look at the very well-defined time period—the 18 months spent serving as Prince Harald's children's nurse—that are documented here, in Inga Berg's journal.

The handwritten Journal is reproduced and accompanied by an English translation with footnotes explaining the people, places and events in her journal. Her handwriting is clear and her usage of Norwegian very direct. The translation is not literal but is in American style English, since the book is intended primarily for American readers. As one would expect in a diary format, many sentence fragments appear as a way to simplify notations. Inga added an interesting feature to her journal with her own personal photographs along with newspaper articles, especially clippings from *Tidens Tegn.*[1] These clippings and other newspaper articles provide complementary information to fill in some of the gaps in her journal.

The *Dagbok* reveals that as a children's nurse, Inga was concerned with Prince Harald's health, and one important indicator—his weight. She frequently commented on his diet along with his general physical condition, level of activity and sleep. She also included comments about his two sisters, Princesses Ragnhild and Astrid. Weather is mentioned often. She notes the many visitors, family trips and travels of Prince Olav and Princess Märtha.

Inga's duties included:

- Practical tasks: Supervising three children, feeding, bathing, walking, and changing clothes
- Overseeing medical and health concerns
- Teaching: crawling and walking, songs, first words and phrases, stories and nursery rhymes, hide and seek
- Coordination: medical with Dr. Frölich, food with the chef/kitchen staff, general schedule with the Royal Family, security issues with Major Østgaard
- Preparation: Baptism of the Prince; parties and receptions; receiving visitors; public outings; coordination for travel, both local and abroad
- Record-keeping: Daily milk intake, daily weight recording, journal writing
- Royal Family time with children: Play time with Prince Harald and his sisters, public functions at the Royal Palace and *Bygdøy Kongsgaard,* family and friends' visits

---

[1] *Tidens Tegn* (Sign of the Times) was an Oslo newspaper reporting extensively on the Royal Family and the arts in the Oslo area. It is no longer being published. To refer to this newspaper, Inga uses the abbreviation T.T.

[Inga Arrives At Skaugum, March 10, 1937]

*Future King/Heir Apparent, Prince Harald[2]
Born February 21 at 12:45 P.M. Weight at
time of birth: 3,170 grams (7 pounds)
Length: 52 cm. (20 inches)[3]*

1937

March 10, 1937

*I came here to Skaugum[4] today on the 10th
at 11:30 A.M. Was very excited to see the
Prince; had been told that he was very hand-
some. He was truly the most beautiful [child]
I've ever seen and I was completely taken with
him the first time I cared for him and held
him in my arms. Mrs. Koren was here when
I arrived, but left later that evening. Princess
Ragnhild and Princess Astrid were very
delightful and helped me unpack, so that was
done in no time. Miss Kiær is very nice and
sweet![5] [Cont.]*

[2] *Arveprins* is translated as future king or heir presumptive.
Inga often refers to Prince Harald using a family nickname,
Lillebror (Little Brother), rather than using royal titles.

[3] One gram equals .035 ounce; 1,000 grams (1 kilogram)
equals about 2.2 pounds. One centimeter equals .39 inch;
2.54 centimeters equal one inch. In temperature, to convert
Celsius, the formula is F degrees = 9/5C + 32.

[4] The Skaugum estate is located on a high ridge above the
Oslo Fjord in an attractive rural setting. Today it is used as a
residence of the next in line to the throne, i.e. the crown
prince or crown princess.

[5] Mrs. Annie Krogh Koren (1900-1960) was *overjordmor*
(director) of midwife programs at *Kvinneklinikken* at the
Rikshospitalet, the most prestigious hospital in Norway.
Mrs. Koren was also Inga's supervisor when she was in the
midwife program. Koren helped deliver Prince Harald along
with Professor Dr. Anton Sunde who was a distinguished
obstetrician at the State Hospital. Midwife Koren took care
of Prince Harald for his first 17 days until Inga replaced her.
Miss Kiær was a live-in housekeeper. At the time of Harald's
birth, his sisters, Princesses Astrid and Ragnhild, were five
and six, respectively.

Onsdag morgen **Aftenposten** 31. mars 1937

Arriving at the East Railway Station for Harald's
baptism were, from left to right: King Haakon, Prince
Carl (Märtha's father), Princess Ingeborg (Märtha's
mother) with Ingeborg's daughter, Margarethe and
Crown Prince Olav in a top hat. In the background was
King Gustaf's representative, *Riksmarskalk Vennersten*
(Head of Palace Household). In addition to rail lines, a
flotilla of ocean-going craft furnished transportation
for various royals and government officials attending
Prince Harald's baptism.

3/te mars 1937.

Prins Harald døpes idag. Efter Kongens uttrykkelige ønske vil dåben foregå i all enkelhet. Kantor

S a n d v o l d fra Vår Frelsers kirke vil spille, damekoret synger og klokkeren og kirketjeneren som assisterer, er likeledes utlånt fra Vår Frelsers kirke.

Man kan gå ut fra at lille prins Harald vil bli døpt i den samme kjole som prinsesse Ragnhild og Astrid engang var iført, og som hans mor og alle prins Carl og prinsesse Ingeborgs andre barn og barnebarn er blitt døpt i.

Der er likeledes all sannsynlighet for at dronning M a u d efter gammel norsk skikk vil bære sin sønnesønn til dåben. Hennes Majestet holdt som bekjent både prinsesse Ragnhild og Astrid over døpefonten, mens prisesse I n g e b o r g løsnet kniplingshetten fra dåbsbarnets hode.

Dåbshøitideligheten begynner presis klokken 12 og foretas av biskop L u n d e. Ca. 200 personer vil være tilstede i Slottskapellet.

Med det ordinære Stockholms-

tog igåraftes kom kongefamiliens svenske gjester til prinsedåben.

Forts. side 2, spalte 4.

[Newspaper article]

Prince Harald will be baptized today. In accordance with the King's explicit wishes, the baptism will be an informal event. Cantor Sandvold from Our Savior's (Vår Frelsers) Church will play,[6] the women's choir will sing, and the sexton and usher who will be assisting will also be provided by Vår Frelsers Church.

Presumably little Prince Harald will wear the same baptismal gown that Princesses Ragnhild and Astrid once wore, and that his mother and all of Prince Carl's and Princess Ingeborg's other children and grandchildren wore at their baptisms.[7]

It is also most likely that Queen Maud, in accordance with old Norwegian traditions, will carry her grandson to the baptism. Her Majesty also carried Princesses Astrid and Ragnhild while they were baptized, while Princess Ingeborg took off their baptismal caps.

The ceremony will begin at noon and Bishop Lunde[8] will conduct the service. About 200 guests will be present at Slottskapellet (the Palace Chapel).[9]

The royal family's Swedish guests arrived on the regular train from Stockholm last evening.

Continued, page 2 column 4. [Probably from Oslo Dagbladet, no date]

[6] Cantor Arild Edvin Sandvold (1895-1984) was organist and choir director at Our Savior's Church (*Vår Frelsers*), now more commonly known as the Cathedral Church (*Domkirken*), located in downtown Oslo near the Oslo Central Train Station (*Sentralstasjon*) at the end of Karl Johans Gate.

[7] Prince Carl of Sweden and Princess Ingeborg of Denmark were the parents of Crown Princess Märtha.

[8] Bishop Johan Peter Lunde 1866-1938 was Bishop of Oslo from 1923-1937. He played an important role in the royal family. Bishop Lunde married Crown Prince Olav and Crown Princess Märtha and baptized all three of their children. He wrote several monographs, including *Jesus fra Nasaret* (Jesus from Nazareth), published in 1930.

[9] The Palace Chapel is attached to the main Palace and seats about 200 people. In addition to regular church services, it is used by the Royal Family for official events like baptisms, weddings and confirmations. The Chapel is also used for concerts.

March, 1937

[10th Cont.] Professor Frölich was also here and gave me advice on what the baby should eat, and then he examined the Prince.[10]
Luckily, Prince Harald is healthy and loves to eat so he will be big and strong.
He was baptized in Slottskapellet *(Royal Palace Chapel). He screamed quite a lot.*
The circumstances were quite unusual for him.

[Newspaper article]

I hope you were listening to the radio the day the Prince cried, I mean, was baptized.
Everybody said it was a solemn moment, even though no one could hear what Bishop Lunde was saying. But we've heard him speak so many times before, that it doesn't really matter.
It was, however, the first time we've heard a Norwegian Prince cry on the radio. I wonder if the nanny pinched him to get him to cry.
From Dagbladet, *Thursday, May 13, [1937].*

[10] Professor Theodor Christian Brun Frölich (1870-1947) was the pediatrician responsible for the medical care of Prince Harald. He specialized in pediatrics and was Professor of Medicine at Oslo University. Also he was active in experimental studies and wrote extensively in the *Journal of Hygiene,* and authored a textbook for Scandinavian doctors specializing in pediatrics.

Proffessor Frölich var her også og ga besked om hvad prinsen skulle spise og undersökte han. Han er heldigvis sund og frisk og glad i mat så snart blir han stor og sterk. Han blev döpt i Slottskapellet. Han skrek nokså meget. Det blev nokså mange ting med stellet og det hele som var anderledes end han var vant til.

Jeg håper du hørte efter i radioen den dagen prinsen skrek, jeg mener blev døpt. Alle sa det var en høitidsstund, enda det var umulig å høre hvad biskop Lunde sa, men han har vi hørt så ofte før at det var ikke så nøie, mens det derimot er første gang en norsk prins har skreket i radioen. Jeg undres på om barnepiken knep ham for å få det til. Dagbladet Torsdag 13de Mai

RINS HARALDS DÅ
enestående vakker høitidelighet i Slottskapellet ida

The baptismal ceremony took place in *Slottskapellet* (The Royal Palace Chapel) with Bishop Lunde, Queen Maud and Princess Ingeborg at the baptismal font and the rest of the Royal Family on the left. Other sponsors *in absentia* were King George of England, Dowager Queen Mary, King Leopold of Belgium and Crown Princess Ingrid of Denmark.

35

Prins Harald var ute på verandaen første gang 4 uker gammel. Han smilte tevist første gang da han var 1 måned.

Den 20 april.
Prins Harald har vært så søt og blid idag. For første gang forsøkte han og snakke litt til oss. Været er stygt med tåke & regn, han er ikke ute idag.

21 de april.
I dag fint vær, så prinsen var ute igjen. Melken minker for; nu får han bare 1 måltid av sin mor.

22 de April.
Regn idag igjen. Harald ligger for åpent vindue. Han var så blid idag. Lå og lekte

---

April. 1937.

med fingrene sine.

24 de april
Prinsen er søt og blid idag; men han hoster lit Håper at han ikke får en forkjølelse.

29 de
Lillebror er bra nu og står på verandaen i strålende solskin. Jeg har tat bilder av ham & prinsessene idag

30 de
Har tat bilder av prinsen idag. Han blir sikkert søt.

1 de Mai
Strålende var. Prins Harald har stått på verandaen i 3 timer Prinsesse Ragnhild tok bilder av ham.

4 de Mai
Kongen er her og leker med prinsessene. Prins Harald sover.

April, 1937

Prince Harald was on the terrace for the first time when he was four weeks old. He smiled for the first time when he was one month old.

20th

Harald has been so sweet and happy today. For the first time, he tried to talk to us a little bit. The weather is bad with both fog and rain, he was not outside today.

21st

The weather is nice, so the Prince was outside again today. The mother's milk is drying up, and now he only gets one meal from his mother.

22nd

It's raining again today. Harald was lying by an open window.[11] He was so happy. He just lay there and played [Cont.]

[11] In Norway, children are given many opportunities to be out in the fresh air. Babies are wrapped in sheepskin sleeping bags and are kept very warm in the coldest weather.

[22nd Cont.] with his fingers.

24th

The Prince was sweet and happy today, but he was coughing a bit. Hope he doesn't catch a cold.

29th

Lillebror[12] is well again now, and he's out on the terrace in the nice spring sun. I've taken pictures of him and the Princesses today.

30th

I've taken more pictures of Lillebror. I'm sure he'll look cute in them.

May, 1937

1st

Great weather today. Harald has been on the terrace for three hours. Princess Ragnhild took pictures of him.

4th

The King is here playing with the Princesses. Prince Harald is sleeping.

[12] This is Inga's first use in her journal of the family nickname, "Little Brother".

[*Barnetoget* (Children's Parade), May 17]

6th

Heavy fog today. Lillebror *is sleeping inside. The King has stopped by again today to greet him and the Princesses.*

8th

Began giving Harald 1 teaspoon cod-liver oil today.[13] Beautiful sunshine. I've taken two pictures of him.

9th

Nasty and cold weather again today. The Prince woke up crying at midnight last night, but he usually sleeps until 4:00 A.M.. He now weighs 4,830 grams.

17th

Rain. Prince Harald must be inside today. The Princesses and I went to the Royal Palace[14] to watch the Children's Parade from the balcony, in the pouring rain.[15]

18th

Good weather. Lillebror *is outside. He now weighs 5,130 grams.*

[13] Cod-liver oil, rich in vitamins A and D, is made from the liver of Norway's national fish, *torsk* (cod); it was and still is used in Norway to prevent serious disease in children. A 1935 publication of the U.S Department of Labor recommends the use of cod-liver oil and many of the same procedures that Inga uses throughout the *Dagbok. (The Child from One to Six,* GPO, number 30)

[14] The Royal Palace *(Det Kongelige Slott),* completed in 1849, was built to serve as the residence for the Swedish king when he was in Norway. The Royal Palace with 158 rooms provided facilities for official receptions and was a comparatively small palace by European standards but nonetheless one with richly decorated interiors.

[15] The Children's Parade *(Barnetoget)* is held every May 17, Constitution Day. Children come to the Royal Palace from all around Oslo in order to march with their banners along Karl Johans Gate. They pass in review before the Royal Family who stand on the Palace balcony waving at the children as they pass.

Crown Prince Olav and Crown Princess Märtha held Prince Harald on the palace balcony.

Oslo, onsdag 18. mai 1938 | Abonn.pr

VER NASJONALDAGE

Barnetoget (Children's Parade) was first started in 1870 and is still held yearly on May 17. The traditional Oslo procession goes up Karl Johans Gate to the Royal Palace.

Mai. 1937.

21 de. Været litt bedre idag men tildels overskyet. Prins Harald står på verandaen. Han er blid og snill om dagen og sover til kl. 4-5 om morgenen. Han veier 5190 gr. og får 2 teskeer tran og 2 t. apelsinsaft pr. dag.

23 de. Fin-fint vær. Lillebror ute hele dagen fra kl. 8 idag. H. M. Kongen var her både igår og idag, men Prinsen sov idag. Har fått 1 bilde av Prinsessene.

24 de. Overskyet, men han er ute idag og er strålende blid. Sover godt om natten til ca kl. 5 idag.

25 de. Lillebror sov til kl. 5.30 idag. og han veier 5310 gr. Han trives utmerket. Kongen var her idag. Vi hörte Kronprinsens tale i

21st

The weather is a little better, but partly cloudy. Prince Harald is out on the balcony. He is happy and good-natured and sleeps until 4:00 or 5:00 A.M. He now weighs 5,190 grams and gets two teaspoons of cod-liver oil and two of orange juice every day.

23rd

Beautiful weather. Lillebror has been outside since 8:00 A.M. King Haakon was here both yesterday and today, but the Prince was sleeping today. I took a picture of the Princesses.

24th

Cloudy, but he's still outside today and in a great mood. Sleeps well at night and slept until 5:00 A.M. this morning.

25th

Lillebror slept until 5:30 A.M., and now weighs 5,310 grams. He is doing great. The King was here today. We heard the Crown Prince speak [Cont.]

Princess Ragnhild, age eight, and Princess Astrid, age six, walk in the Skaugum garden with Crown Prince Harald.

May, 1937

[25nd Cont.] on the radio in connection with the opening of the Norwegian pavilion [at the World's Fair] in Paris.[16] Ragnhild cried.

26th

Fog in the morning. Beautiful weather after 1:00 P.M. The Prince was outside all day.

27th

Rain. The painters are whitewashing both terraces, so the Prince had to be inside. Fog and rain.

28th

Sunny, but very windy. Prince Harald now weighs 5,370 grams. His digestion is fine, as usual, and he's happy and content. The Crown Prince couple [Olav and Märtha] came home from Paris and King Haakon came over for dinner.

29th

A bit of sun, harsh wind, and unpleasant weather. Prince outside until 4:00 P.M.

30th

Stormy outside. We stayed inside. I took a picture of the Prince.

[16] It was important for a young country, 32 years as an independent nation, to be part of this prestigious event. World's Fairs are usually held in major cities with no set national rotation, and include International expositions of the arts, crafts, scientific advances, industrial and agricultural products. Paris was the site of the World's Fair in May 1937, called by the French: *Exposition Internationale des Arts et des Techniques dans la vie Moderne* (International Exposition of the Arts and Sciences in Modern Life).

The Crown Princess was thrilled to have given birth to Prince Harald. "I was indeed unfulfilled until I had a son," she said to Inga. (*Oppland Arbeiderblad*, May 12, 1979)

Inga holding baby Harald when he was two months old. She is quoted in a Bagn area newspaper, *Oppland Arbeiderblad*, 1979: "What I was most excited about was to be able to hold a real Prince in my arms."

Juni. 1937.

1ste
Strålende sol fra morgenen; men regn utpå dagen. Lille-bror ute fra kl. 8 morgen. Prinsesse-ne har vært ute for å fiske; men fik ingen fisk. Nu er de ute med „Stjernen" og ser på Regatta.

2den
Stygt vær med torden & regnbyger Sol imellem. Prinsen er inde og er like blid & fornöiet.

3die
Sol; men kald vind. Tat bilde av prinsen og mig. Han skrek.

5te
Regn og surt. Prinsessene er i Oslo og ser på Osloprinsessen. Jeg kjörte inn med kronprinsparret.

6te
Regn og tåke. Prins Harald inne hele dagen. Vegt. 5560 gr.

June, 1937

1st

Beautiful sun in the morning, but some rain in the afternoon. Lillebror *was outside from 8:00 in the morning. The Princesses have been out fishing, but they didn't catch anything. Now they're out aboard* Stjernen *watching the Regatta.[17]*

2nd

Thunder and rain today. Sun from time to time. Prince Harald is inside and happy just the same.

3rd

Sun, but cold wind. Took a picture of the Prince and me. He cried.

5th

Rain and nasty weather. The princesses are in Oslo looking at the Oslo [festival] princess.[18] I drove in with the Crown Prince couple.
*[As part of the festival each year they chose an Oslo Princess (*Osloprinsessen*). The festival is no longer held in Oslo.]*

6th

Rain and fog. Prince Harald was inside all day. Weight 5,560 grams.

[17] Upon Norwegian independence in 1905, *Stjernen* (The Star), the Royal Norwegian Yacht, was given to King Haakon VII by its previous owner, King Oscar II of Sweden. Many members of the Royal Family have been avid sailors, especially King Olav V; and ship racing is part of Norwegian culture.

[18] Beginning in 1933 Oslo Day *(Oslodagen)* was initiated by the Director *(Turistsjef)* of the Oslo Tourist Board, Alfhild Hovdan.

Prince Harald posed on a blanket in the Skaugum garden in the summer of 1937.

June, 1937

7th

Student singers from Latvia were here today and they sang a lullaby dedicated to Prince Harald.[19] He sat in my arms, by the window, listening. Nice weather.

8th

Cloudy weather. Prince Harald and the Princesses were photographed by a number of photographers today.

9th

Princess Ragnhild's birthday is today.[20] Fog in the morning, but after that, the weather was nice. Count Folke Bernadotte, 5 years old, is staying here with his nanny.[21] Today, everyone is gathered at Bygdøy Kongsgård (Bygdøy King's Farm).[22] The Queen is hosting the party. Prince Harald got his first vaccine shot today.

10th

I'm leaving to go on vacation for 14 days today. Nice weather.

24th

Came home from vacation today. [Cont.]

[19] Latvia, a Baltic neighbor and fellow Lutheran nation, is well known for its church choirs.

[20] This was the seventh birthday of Princess Ragnhild, [born June 9, 1930].

[21] Count Folke Bernadotte was the son of Folke Bernadotte, Sr., a descendent of the founder of the House of Bernadotte and the famous Napoleonic Marshal, Jean-Baptiste who was born in Pau, France. The original Bernadotte improved his Swedish credentials by changing his name to Karl Johan when he succeeded to the Norwegian-Swedish throne in 1818, giving rise to the name of Oslo's famous street, Karl Johans Gate.

[22] *Bygdøy Kongsgard* (the King's farm on Bygdøy Island) has been called the best-known farm in Norway. Although it is close to downtown Oslo, the farm is still in full agricultural production. *Bygdøy,* formerly an island, is now a peninsula of over two square miles. King Olav V used nearby *Oscarshall Slott* (Oscar's Castle) as a summer residence. *Oscarshall* is now a museum open to the public. The residence on the King's farm underwent a complete renovation from 2003 to 2007; King Harald and Queen Sonja began using it in 2008.

Crown Princess Märtha and Prince Harald smile at each other.

Juni 1937

Kort visit på Hovslagargatan.

Det var som man kan förstå rätt livligt nere på Centralen i morse.

När tåget rullade in stodo prinsessan Ingeborg och prins Carl j:r på perrongen för att ta emot det kärkomna besöket. Det blev naturligtvis omfamningar i långa banor, och småprinsessorna visade särskild glädje över att få träffa mormor igen.

Men för deras del blev uppehållet i Stockholm inte långvarigt. Man hann knappast komma upp på Hovslagaregatan förrän det var att sätta sig i bilen igen och åka ned till Centralen, ty precis åtta skulle tåget till Fridhem gå. Prins Haralds säng i näpnaste ljusblått stuvades in i en förstaklasskupé, och syskonen hjälpte barnsköterskan att se till att han blev ordentligt nedbäddad. Så blev det stora kramen till mamma innan tåget rullade söderut.

Kronprinsessan Märtha stannar kvar i Stockholm till i eftermiddag, då hon bilar ned till Fridhem tillsammans med prinsessan Ingeborg och prins Carl j:r.

Kronprins Olav kommer litet senare. Nu är han upptagen av att deltaga i några segeltävlingar.

26de Juni

Short visit at Hovslagargatan[23]

It was understandably an exciting atmosphere at the train station this morning. As the train came in, Princess Ingeborg and Prince Carl stood ready to greet the visitors. It was of course a joyful reunion, and the little girls were especially happy to see their grandmother again. But the Princesses did not stay for long. They had barely arrived at Hovslagargatan before they had to return to the train station again, and continue on to Fridhem.[24] Prince Harald's beautiful blue bed was loaded into a first class sleeping car, and his sisters helped his nanny get him to bed. The Princesses were clinging to their mother until the train began its journey south. Crown Princess Märtha will be staying in Stockholm until this afternoon, when she will drive to Fridhem with Princess Ingeborg and Prince Carl Jr. Crown Prince Olav will be arriving later. He is currently busy as a participant in sailboat races.

[Probably from the Stockholm newspaper, Dagens Nyheter; the text being in Swedish, n.d, circa June 26, 1937.]

[23] On Skeppsholmen Island, Hovslagargatan is a street which is very close to Blasieholmen which runs along the back of the *Moderna Museet* (Modern Museum) in Stockholm.

[24] Fridhem is the ancestral family estate of Swedish Crown Princess Märtha; it was bought and built by her father, Prince Carl, Sr. Fridhem is located 90 miles southwest of Stockholm by train.

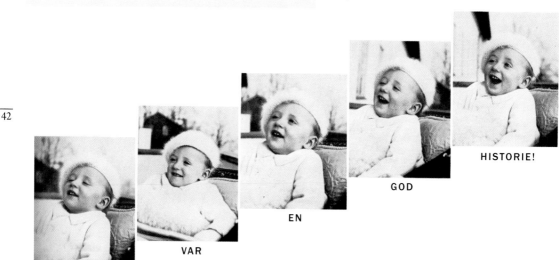

DET VAR EN GOD HISTORIE!

June, 1937

[24th Cont.] It has rained a lot. The Prince has gained weight, and now weighs 5,850 grams. Doesn't get cod-liver oil anymore.

[Trip to Fridhem and Stockholm, Sweden, June 25 - July 13, 1937]

25th

Leaving today for Fridhem in Sweden. The Prince was in high spirits. There was a huge crowd at the train station, who took pictures of him and filmed him. [He ate] one-half orange.

26th

Arrived in Stockholm at 6 A.M.[25] The Prince slept through the whole night and is happy and content. There were photographers here as well. We had breakfast at Prince Carl's, before going on to Fridhem by train. It's very beautiful and nice here, but I'm so tired, I can barely keep my eyes open. [I] didn't sleep last night.

27th

Today was a [Cont.]

[25] There is no direct rail line to Fridhem, so it is necessary to first travel from Oslo to Stockholm, and then on to Fridhem, thus adding to total travel time.

Crown Princess Märtha's family estate is called Fridhem (home of peace).

As is evident in her *Dagbok*, Inga took meticulous care of Prince Harald. She commented on his health many times: "He was almost never sick and was brought up to enjoy spending time in the fresh air."

Juni 1937.

varm og strålende dag. Prinsen
har stått i parken i hele dag.
Han har også solet sig lit.
Jeg sluttet med han igår, gir
ham bare apelsinsaft nu.
Han trives så bra.

28de

Prinsessene er på bil & fisketur
med kong Gustav. idag. Det er
så stille efter dem. Prinsen
stod i parken fra kl. 10-5¹⁵ idag.
Han skrek endel & var urolig.
Nu sover han godt. Det har
vært en varm & herlig dag.

29de.

Idag regner det også her
prinsen stod på verandaen
til kl. 4 em. da beg. regnet.

30de

Litt regn også idag. Lillebror veier nu
5960gr. Prinsesse Margaretha kom idag.

June, 1937

[27th Cont.] warm and beautiful day. The Prince has been out in the park, all day, also sunning himself a bit. I stopped giving him cod-liver oil yesterday; he only gets orange juice now. He's having a great time here.

28th

King Gustav[26] took the Princesses for a ride in the car, and then they went fishing. It's quiet here without them. The Prince was outside in the park today from 10:00 A.M. to 5:15 P.M., and he cried some. But right now, he's sleeping quietly. It's been a warm and lovely day.

29th

Today it's raining here too, but the Prince was out on the terrace until 4:00 P.M. when it started to rain.

30th

A bit of rain today too. Lillebror now weighs 5,960 grams. Princess Margrethe[27] came to visit today.

[26] King Gustav V, King of Sweden, lived until age 92 (1858-1950). His wife, Queen Victoria, was of German background. There was concern during World War II that the Queen may have influenced the King in favor of Germany.

[27] Princess Margrethe was a sister of Crown Princess Märtha.

Inga, in her official nurse's uniform, held Prince Harald before beginning one of their outings.

July, 1937

1st

Pretty nice weather today, sun and rain. The Prince was outside until 1:00 P.M. today, when it started to rain. He's a bit crabby today.

2nd

Nice weather. The Prince has gotten a little sunburned and is crying quite a bit.

3rd

Beautiful weather. The Crown Princess is in Stockholm. Lillebror is good.

4th, Sunday.

Still beautiful weather. The kids, Annie[28], and I moved to Captain von Dyrssen's[29] house this afternoon.

5th

Prince Harald is just as happy, regardless of how much we move around, in fact, he seems to like the change.

[28] Miss Annie Butler was an English tutor for the Princesses and was the former nurse for Olav when they were living in England. Queen Maud brought her along to Norway and later asked her back to continue her service as tutor in the English language.

[29] Captain von Dyrssen was in the Swedish military, and as a friend of Prince Carl (the father of Princess Märtha), he moved in the elite circles of Sweden.

July, 1937

6th

Prince Carl's wedding.[30] The Princesses were in church during the ceremony; afterward Lillebror, the Princesses and I went back to Fridhem. The Prince was good-natured and nice as usual. Afterwards we took a swim, lovely water, but a little cold at first.

7th

The Princesses, Sister Elna,[31] and I went swimming twice today, lovely water. Lillebror lay upstairs and slept. Afterwards, we traveled back to Fridhem.

8th

The Prince and I have been in the park all day, very hot.

9th

Thunder and rain showers, [Cont.]

[30] Prince Carl Jr. was Crown Princess Märtha's brother; he married Countesse Elsa von Rosen.

[31] Sister Elna was a Swedish nurse on the staff of the Swedish Royal Family and occasionally assisted nurse Inga. [Note the spelling of Norwegian "søster" and Swedish spelling "syster" in the journal.]

Juli 1937.

9de
tummert. Prinsen står inne
sol; men utrygt. Grev & grevinne
10de   Bonde har vært her.
Varmt og sol. Lillebror har stått i
parken hele dagen. Var i dag-
morges i besök i vaskeriet med
ham. De syntes han var söt
Kaptein & fru Dyrssen vært
her for lunch. – Vi fikk for
lunch idag: Avsilet ertersuppe
kold kylling med tomater og
grönne erter, jordbær med flöte
11de
Prinsen sovet i hele dag
og jeg pakku så det er
rigtig deilig han er så snill
Kronprinsen og kronprinsessen
reiste til Stockholm allerede
idag. Vi reiser imorgen.
Det har regnet rigtig godt

July, 1937

[9th Cont.] *very humid. The Prince stayed inside. Weather sunny but unstable. Count and Countess Bonde came to visit.*[32]

10th

Warm and sunny. Lillebror *has been in the park all day. We visited the workers at Fridhem's laundry this morning. Everyone thought he was quite the charmer. Captain and Mrs. [Von] Dyrssen were here for lunch. Today's lunch consisted of pea soup, cold chicken with tomatoes and green peas, and strawberries with cream.*

11th

The Prince has slept all day, which is nice, because I have a lot of packing to do.
The Crown Prince couple went to Stockholm today. We're leaving tomorrow. It's been raining a lot [Cont.]

[32] The Bondes were friends of the parents of Crown Princess Märtha and were members of the Swedish nobility.

Inga Berg, Princesses Astrid and Ragnhild, one of the Von Dyrssen's daughters, and Miss Annie Butler, the English tutor for the sisters, were shown here at the Von Dyrssen's mansion. Note that Annie Butler is wearing two medals presented to her by King Haakon in recognition of her long service to the Royal Family.

Harald demonstrated that he is "so big" to his approving mother.

July, 1937

[11th Cont.] today, but the sun came out in the afternoon.

12th

Traveled to Count Bernadotte's[33] home in Stockholm today, and stayed there with the Bernadottes and their children for a little while. Okye,[34] his "dada" [child's name for nurse], the Princesses and I were at Skansen.[35] We left from the station at 10:05 P.M. for home.

13th

The Prince slept through the night on the train. We got up when the train reached Lillestrøm,[36] not a single person in sight at the station. The King met us at Østbanen,[37] where a huge crowd showed up to see the Prince. He was good while we were traveling, but he's been crying a lot since we got home. Nice weather here too. [Cont.]

[33] Folke Bernadotte's wife Estelle was an American.

[34] *Okye* appears to be a baby name for Åke Bernadotte.

[35] *Skansen* is the oldest open-air museum in the world. Founded in 1891, it depicts the ways of life in different parts of Sweden.

[36] Lillestrøm is a city located on the rail line east of Oslo.

[37] The old East Railroad Station (*Østbanestasjonen*) was located in the east end of downtown Oslo and is now called *Sentralstasjonen*.

July, 1937

[13th Cont.] The King [Haakon VII], the Queen [Maud], and two English ladies were here for tea. The Prince was shown off for a little while, and he was so cute. All the guests came upstairs to watch him take a bath. Weight: 6,175 grams.

22nd

We moved here to Bygdøy Kongsgård yesterday. The Crown Prince couple went to Bodø[38]. The Queen is so proud of Harald, she had two ladies over for tea today in order to show him off. He is really magnificent. He seemed a bit restless today and had off-color stools. He's been eating bananas and rusks[39] for four days now. Maybe [Cont]

[38] Bodø is a coastal town of 32,000 people at the northern end of the Nordland railroad line. The town is known for its herring fisheries.

[39] Rusks, a common daily food for teething babies, are made from sweetened, raised bread, then sliced and toasted in an oven or baked a second time, browned and made crisp. Many families add cinnamon for more flavor.

Juli 1937.

23de

mindre vel, ellers er det tan-
ner, han suger på fingeren
hele dagen nu. og sikler.
til lunch i dag fik vi: avkokt
laks med salad, kylling med
spinat og blomkål. Vaniljeis-
mous, jordbær med fløte og
frukt.

25de

Prinsen står i parken her hele
dagen. De to første dagene
var han svært urolig og hadde litt grønn og slimet av-
føring også; men idag er
han heldigvis helt bra igjen
I eftermiddag var han nede
i salongen og lå på teppet
sit og sparket dronningen
som sat ved siden av ham
på knærne. Han var rigtig

Juli 1937.

25de

søt, blid og fornøiet. Hans
vekt er nu 6280 gr. Fint var
med regn og tordenbyger inn-
imellem. — Dronningen er
bedårende søt og hyggelig
og helt betat av prins Harald.
Har har nu 1 uke fåt litt banan og kavringgrøt. Han liker det.

31te

Her har vært strålende vær
hele uken, og jeg har vært
med prinsessene og badet de
siste 4 dage. I morgen kommer
frk. Lewi og skal bade med
oss. Prins Harald har skreket
og vært urolig i flere dage
i dag morges skrek han i
1½ time; men da fikk
han også sin første tann
og jeg fik en nydelig nål

July, 1937

23rd [Cont] it doesn't agree with him or it might be due to his teething because he keeps sucking his fingers and drooling all day. For lunch today we got boiled salmon with salad, chicken with spinach and cauliflower, vanilla mousse, strawberries with heavy cream, and fruit.

25th

The Prince was out in the park all day. The first two days he was a little restless, and his stools were also off color. But now, fortunately, he's back to normal. This afternoon he was lying on his blanket down in the drawing room, and he kicked the Queen who was kneeling next to him. He was [Cont.]

July, 1937

[25th Cont.] sweet, happy, and content. He now weighs 6,280 grams. Nice weather with some rain and thunder from time to time. The Queen is so sweet and nice, and completely taken with Prince Harald. He's been getting some bananas, and porridge made from bananas and crushed rusks this past week. He likes it.

31st

We've had fabulous weather all week, and I've been swimming with the Princesses for the past four days. Tomorrow Miss Lewi[40] will come swimming with us. Prince Harald has been cranky and crying a lot for several days now. This morning he screamed for an hour and a half, but that was because he was getting his first tooth. The Queen gave me a beautiful pin [Cont.]

[40] Miss Lewi was an on-call nurse for the children at Skaugum.

July, 1937

[July 31 Cont.] with two pearls and a ruby set in gold. The King and Queen have both been so nice. The Prince has been in the drawing room for about 45 minutes each afternoon. Aftenposten[41] was here and took a lot of pictures of the Queen and the Princesses and the Prince. They were in the newspaper today and looked wonderful. The Queen was so beautiful and the children were so cute.

August, 1937

1st

We left Bygdøy Kongsgård *today. The Crown Prince couple came (home) from Røros[42] and were delayed as usual, so we didn't arrive at Skaugum until 6:30 P.M. The Prince was in good spirits the entire day.*

[41] *Aftenposten* (Evening Mail), a conservative Oslo newspaper, is the largest in Norway.

[42] Røros is an old copper mining town in Sør-Trøndelag, located about 400 miles northeast of Oslo, not far from the Swedish border.

August, 1937

2nd

Prince Harald probably got really spoiled at Kongsgården, since we pushed him around the park in his buggy all day long. Today he's been on the terrace and crying all day. Miss Butler [Annie Butler was the English tutor for the Princesses] is so angry, and thinks I'm terrible for letting him cry like that; she forgets that it's hardest on me.

8th

The Prince now weighs 6,490 grams, and gets 850 grams of fluids, 1 banana, 1 whole rusk, and the juice from 1 orange. Rain and thunder today. Before that, the weather was nice for a whole week. Major Østgaard[43] and his wife were here for lunch today. The children go swimming every day with the Crown Prince couple.

[43] *Oberst* (Colonel) Nikolai Ramm Østgaard (1885-1955) was an *aide-de-camp* (equerry and manager of the Skaugum estate) of Crown Prince Olav and had his own office at Skaugum. He was a cross-country ski coach and Chair of the Norwegian Ski Association. Later when Prince Harald was 15, Østgaard instructed him in cross-country skiing. During World War II he accompanied Crown Prince Olav to England, Scotland, the United States and Canada. *Oberst* Østgaard received many medals from King Haakon including the Commander of the Star of the Order of St. Olav.

Juli 1937.

31.te
med 2 perler og 1 rubin i gull. Kongen og dronningen har vært så søte og hyggelige og Prinsen har vært nede i salongen hver em. ca. 3 kvarter. Aftenposten var her og tokk en hel del bilder av Dronningen og prinsessene og prinsen. De stod i avisen for idag og var riktig pene. Dronningen var så pen og barna var så søte.

1ste August.
Vi reiste idag fra Bygdøy Kongsgård idag. Kronprins-parret som kom fra Røras av som sedvanlig forsinket så vi kom hertil Skaugum først kl. 6.30 em. Prinsen var søt og snill hele tiden.

August 1937.

2.den
Prinsen er blit riktig bort-skjemt på Kongsgården for vi kjørte ham rundt i parken i barnevogn, hele dagen, så idag da han har stått på verandaen har han skreket hele tiden og miss Butler er så sint - og synes jeg er gru- som som lar ham skrike slik; hun glemmer rent at det jo er verst for mig.

8de
Prinsen veier nu 6490 gr. og får 850 gr. vedske og 1 banan 1 kavring og saften av 1 apelsin. Regn og torden idag. Har vært strålende vær i over en uke nu. Major Østgård og frue her for lunch idag. Barna bader hver dag med kronprinsparret.

12th

Beautiful weather today. Yesterday rain and thunder. The Prince got his first tooth yesterday, and today another one appeared. He gets one whole banana and one rusk and eats it all with a hearty appetite. He's become quite big and chubby. The King and Queen brought guests over for tea. Princess Ragnhild felt ill and vomited. Princess Astrid felt sick yesterday, but she's fine today.

16th

Prince Harald weighs 6,680 grams now. We had both rain and sun intermittently today. The Prince was out on the terrace all day.

[Prince Harald Is Six Months Old, August 21, 1937]

21st

The Prince is six months old today, hale and hearty. He weighs 6,670 grams, so he has [Cont.]

[21st Cont.] not been gaining any weight this week, but he's quite round and chubby. He's good-natured, although he does cry once in a while, just like other children.

27th

Professor Frölich was here yesterday, and today I'm feeding the Prince semolina (semulegrynsgrøt).[44] He didn't like it, but then I sang for him and it all went down.

28th

We tried feeding the Prince carrot purée today, but he didn't like it.

29th

Lillebror weighs 6,680 grams now. He eats semolina twice a day, different sorts of purée, bananas, rusks, and 600 grams of plain milk. He's not supposed to get any more of the bottle he loves so much. [Cont.]

[44]Semulegrynsgrøt is semolina (middlings of wheat), especially used to make pudding, and is a common baby food.

August, 1937

[29th Cont.] He eats his various porridges and purées with a hearty appetite. He liked tomatoes right away. Photographer Wilse[45] was here on Tuesday and took pictures of him. It must have been hard on him [the Prince], because he was pale and sad when it was all over. His picture will be on the Red Cross Christmas Seal.[46] The Crown Princess traveled to Copenhagen, and will be gone for 14 days. I hope the Prince and the Princesses stay healthy and that they improve both spiritually and physically while she is gone.

[45]Anders Beer Wilse had a studio in Oslo and was one of the best known of the many professional photographers of the Prince and the Royal Family

[46]The Red Cross Christmas Seal (stamp) featured the photograph of the new Prince which was to be sold to raise funds for The Red Cross. Some of the best-trained nurses in Norway were trained in Red Cross hospitals. The Red Cross was founded in Norway in 1865 as the Society for the care of the sick and wounded in the battlefield and for support of the families of those killed. Today the basic principle of the organization is the protection of human life and rights in order to work towards worldwide peace.

Harald saw his lunch on its way.

Photograph of Prince Harald for Christmas Seal Stamp, November 30, 1937.

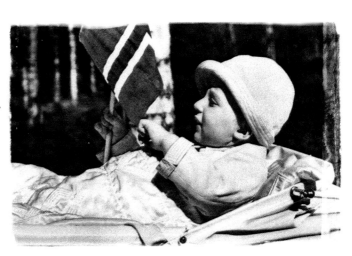

The Prince was taught to wave the Norwegian flag on special occasions.

September 1937

September 37.

1st

Rain and cold. The Prince is not equally fond of all the purées and porridges. He protests loud and clear, but is growing and gaining weight.

11th

The Crown Princess and the Crown Prince came back from Copenhagen today. The Princesses are extremely excited to see them again. **Lillebror** *was in a good mood yesterday and today and he slept well. There have been times when he's been cranky and unhappy. Maybe he misses his bottle, but I've stopped giving [it to] him. He's had a healthy weight increase and now weighs 6,955 grams. His digestive system is also good. Professor Frölich is very pleased with him.*

15th

The Princesses started school today.

September, 1937

21st

Lillebror is seven months old today. He weighs a little over seven kg and is 71 cm tall. He is gentle and good-natured as a rule. He sleeps from 6:30 P.M. to 6:30 A.M. He loves food, but even so he fusses while he is eating. He has been doing this ever since the first time he was given porridge and purées. I hope he gets rid of that habit soon. It's so difficult to feed him when he's crying, coughing, and pushing the food away. The weather has been nice these past couple of days; a little bit of rain once in a while, but otherwise mild and nice.

26th

Beautiful weather. Harald is doing well. Annie [Butler] went back to England today.

[Newspaper Article]

"The Princesses at Skaugum have been given two beautiful alpeluer *(beret-type hat) in fall colors. Prince Harald should not feel left out either. A flower duck was made for him by the blind!"*
From T.T. [Tidens Tegn], *Saturday, October 2,* [1937].

September 1937.

Og to små fortryllende alpeluer i høstfarver er laget til de små prinsesser på Skaugum. Arveprins Harald skal ikke få grunn til å føle sig tilsidesatt heller. En blomsterand er laget til ham. Av de blinde!

T.T. Lördag 2 den Okt.

Inga Berg prepared Crown Prince Harald for his daily walk.

In the summer of 1938, the Prince walked around the Skaugum rose garden by holding onto the *Barnevogn* (baby carriage).

Oktober 1937

3die.

Prins Harald har lagt på sig bare 25 gr. denne uke og veier nu 7285 gr. Han er blid og fornøiet og har heldigvis sluttet med å småskrike når han spiser. Kongen har vært her idag.

11te

Lillebror er så snill og søt om dagen; men igårnat skrek han litt og våknet kl. 5 hvad han ikke har gjort siden han var 3 måneder. Han veier 7375 gr. Kronprinsen + kronprinsessen var bortreist lørdag og søndag, fin, fint vær om dagene.

16de

Lillebror har fått sin 3die tann idag, eller rettere sagt inat. Han er så snill og blid nu det er overstått. Litt smerter

October, 1937

3rd

Prince Harald has gained only 25 grams this week and now weighs 7,285 grams. He's happy and content, and fortunately he no longer fusses when I feed him. King Haakon was here today.

11th

Lillebror has been in a good mood all day, but last night he cried a little and was up at 5:00 A.M. He hasn't done that since he was three months old. He now weighs 7,375 grams. The Crown Prince and the Crown Princess were gone Saturday and Sunday. The weather is beautiful these days.

16th

Lillebror got his third tooth today, or more accurately, last night. He is in such a good mood, now that it's all over with. [Cont.]

Tat Skaugum 31te aug.

PRINS HARALD på julemerke.

NORGES RØDE KORS

Norges Røde Kors presenterer her arveprins Harald på julemerket. Billedet er reprodusert efter fotografi av Wilse.

Merket har fått en meget smukk utførelse og vil sikkert bli flittig brukt på julepakkene. Merket koster 2 øre.

T. T. 1ste nov.

[Newspaper Article]

Taken at Skaugum August 31, [1937]
"Norway's Red Cross has placed Prince Harald's photo on the Christmas Seal. The picture was taken by professional photographer Wilse. The seal is beautifully done and will certainly be widely used on Christmas gifts. It costs two øre."[47]
From T.T., November 1, [1937]

[47] In Norwegian currency: 100 øre = one Norwegian Kroner (NK or Norwegian Crown); in the twentieth and twenty-first centuries the Norwegian Crown has usually fluctuated between five and eight crowns to the U.S. dollar.

The Prince in his stroller

"Prince Harald is the thirty-second generation in direct lineage from our first King, Harald Hårfagre"[48] – this is how the beautiful picture album from Abels Kunstforlag *begins.*[49]
And if the first King could have seen his name-sake in the thirty-second generation, what a proud smile would have spread across his face. And if he could have seen his young descendent crawling around in the green and gorgeous surroundings of Skaugum park, perhaps he would have shaken his famous locks and mumbled admiringly, "Look, look, only six months old and already quite the man!"
The Royal Highness in an embroidered dress, with tiny feet and hands and deep dimples, is a joyous sight; and the two curly-haired blond Princesses beam with adventure in their eyes.
[*Probably from* Tidens Tegn, *circa November 1, 1937*]

Arveprinsen i sin barnevogn.

Arveprins Harald er i 32. ledd er ætling av rikets første konge, Harald Hårfagre — — slik begynner det vakre billedhefte Abels Kunstforlag denne-gang sender ut. Og hadde landets før-ste rikskonge kunnet se sitt navnebarn i 32. ledd, hvilket ættestolt smil hadde ikke bredt sig over heltekongens an-sikt! Og hadde han videre fått nyde synet av sin unge ætling på krypesta-diet i Skaugumparkens sommergrønne omgivelser, hvem vet om han ikke had-de ristet på sin berømmelige hårmanke og anerkjennende mumlet: Se, se, 6 måneder gammel, og allerede meget til kar —!

En kongelig høihet i kjole med legg og broderier, med bare små føtter og hender med dype smilehuller er et syn av intens og betagende ynde, og to lys-lokkete små prinsesser har eventyrets forgjettende glans over sin panne — —

---

[48] Harald *Hårfagre* (Harald the Fairhair) was the first Norwegian King to unify the nation (880-930). [Most Norwegians want to claim lineage from him since he had more than 20 sons. With a very small population at that time, only around 200,000, this claim may have some merit].

[49] *Abels Kunstforlag* is a publisher of high quality artwork.

October, 1937

[*16th Cont.*] *He probably experienced some pain, and he cried for a little while, but not too long. Nice fall weather, pretty mild.*

17th

The Prince isn't gaining as fast as before. He gained only 15 grams last week and now weighs 7,390 grams. He got two new teeth this week. Today he got a new molar, and the second upper incisor is also breaking through. The Crown Prince went to Porsgrunn[50] to see the national soccer match.

18th

Lillebror got his fifth tooth today—that's three teeth in three days. Beautiful weather. 20 degrees [about 68°F] on the terrace in the sun.

21st

Today he's eight months old. The whole household has a cold, and now [*Cont.*]

---

[50] Porsgrunn, renowned for its porcelain factory, is located in the southeast of Norway, about 180 miles from Oslo.

Oktober 1937.
har han nok hat, har skreket
oaen gange; ..... ikke så vænt
meget. Tirs høstvær, ganske mild.
17de
Han legger ikke på sig så
meget som tidligere og veier nu:
7390 gr. altså bare 15 gr. siste uke;
men så har han også fåt 2
tenner denne uke, idag har
han fåt en sidetann, den annen
fortann i overmunn står også i
spretten. Kronprinsen er i Porsgrun
på landskampen idag.
18de
Lillebror fik sin 5te tann
idag altså 3 tenner på 3 dage.
Strålende vær. 20% varme på
verandaen i solen.
21de
Idag er han 8 mnd. Hele
huset er forkjølet og nu har

Oktober 1937

han også desverre beg. å hoste
Det er ikke meget så jeg håper
det går fort over.
23 de Kronprinsparret reiste på
jakt idag, til Torespladsen og blir
borte til søndag. Vekt: _7750 gr._
_30te_
Også idag er kronprinsparret
bortreist, denne gang til Maarud
gård i Odalen til godseier Stang
Lillebror lægger meget på sig
nu og veier idag: _7920 gr._
1ste november.
Dette bilde av Lillebror stod
i avisen idag. Han er helt
bra av sin lille forkjølelse
nu; men han hostet litt
en hel uke. Fikk idag sin
sjette tann og er så blid så blid.

November 1937.

_10de_
Både igår og idag har der vært
fotografer her og tat bilder av
hele familien. Igår Sjøwal, idag
Anderson. – Prinsen veier 8050 gr.
og er lubben og trivelig og
som regel igodt humør; men
skrek idag da han skulle
fotograferes; var svært blid igår.
_14de_
Lillebror veier 8085 gr. og har
7 tenner, fik den 7de tann
den 11te d.s. Jeg tok _5_ bilder
av ham idag i forskjellige
stillinger et med Kronprinsessen
og ham. På de andre var han
alene, det siste hadde han
sin fine skinncape på.
_21de_
Vekt 8145 gr. Ellers ingen
forandringer. Sneslud.

October, 1937

*[21st Cont.] he's starting to cough too.
It's not too bad, so I hope it will pass quickly.*

23rd

*The Crown Prince couple went hunting at
Toresplassen[51] today, and they'll stay there
until Sunday. Weight: 7,750 grams.*

30th

*The Crown Prince couple is gone today too,
traveling to Maarud farm in Odalen.[52]
Lillebror is gaining weight rapidly and today
weighs 7,920 grams.*

November 1

*There was a picture of Lillebror in the paper
today. His cold lasted for a whole week, but he
is completely over it now. Got his sixth tooth
today, and is very happy.*

[51] *Toresplassen* is a hunting lodge not very far from Skaugum
located in a forest called Krokskogen and owned by the
Fearnley/Astrup family.

[52] *Maarud* farm, a famous name of Norwegian dairy products,
is known today for Maarud *potetgull* (potato chips)
(lit. potato gold). Located in the central valley of Odalen, the
farm is about 50 miles northeast of Oslo in Hedmark County.

November, 1937

10th

*There have been photographers here both
yesterday and today—yesterday photographer
Sjøwall, today Anderson[53]—taking pictures of
the entire family. The Prince is quite chubby
and weighs 8,050 grams now. He is usually in
a good mood but cried today when he was
being photographed. [He was] very cheerful
yesterday.*

14th

*Lillebror weighs 8,085 grams now and has
seven teeth; got the seventh tooth on the 11th.
I took five pictures of him today in different
poses, including one with the Crown Princess.
In the rest of the pictures he posed alone, and
in the last one he wore his nice fur jacket.*

21st

*Weight: 8,145 grams. Otherwise no changes.
Sleet.*

[53] Sjøwall and Anderson were Oslo professional photographers.
Gunnar Theodor Sjøwall, grandson, still has a photo atelier/
studio in Oslo on Karl Johans Gate.

December, 1937

<u>2nd</u>

The cabinet members [government administration] and their wives were here for dinner yesterday. Miss Thoren [head housekeeper] and I ate at Østgaards office. We got turtle-soup, pheasant with a salad, mandarin (orange) ice cream with cakes and fruit, Champagne and red wine.

Lillebror is restless at night; maybe he's getting another tooth. He weighs 8,190 grams. He's happy and content in the daytime. It's snowing so much, we almost have a half meter of snow. It's minus 6 degrees [about 20°F] today and a bit of wind. The first snow came about a week ago.

<u>5th</u>

Lillebror weighs 8,325 grams today. We have minus 13 degrees [about + 9°F], but the weather is wonderful. Lillebror stands in front of the open window. There's been a little fog [Cont.]

December, 1937

[5th Cont.] this fall and this winter. The Princesses have a Swedish nurse here now. She came three weeks ago. Lillebror sleeps through the nights again now. I believe he slept too much during the day for a while.

<u>12th</u>

Lillebror weighs [blank]. It's snowing again today. It was cold last night, minus 11 degrees [about + 12°F], now it's only minus five degrees [about +23°F].

<u>15th</u>

The Prince stood up in his crib for the first time today, but he's almost ten months old now.

<u>16th</u>

Lillebror got his eighth tooth today. He's healthy. Ever since infancy his bowels have moved two to three times a day and they continue to do so. [Cont.]

Desember 1937.

2 den.

Igår var regjeringen med damer her i selskap. Frk. Thoren og jeg spiste på Østgårds konto, vi fik: Skilpaddesuppe, en hel urmurit fasan med salad, mandarinis med kaker, frugt & champagne rødvin.

Lillebror er urol g om nettene. Kanske får han en tann til nu. Han veier 8190 gr. Han er blid og snill om dagen. Her sner og snør så nu er den snart ½m. 6 kuldegr. er i dag og litende sno. Det første snefald i år var for ca. 1 uk siden

5te

Lillebror veier 8325 gr idag Her er 13 kuldegrader men stiå-le de vær. Han står for åpent indu. Her har vært lit tåke

---

December 1937.

i høst og vinter. Prinsessene har svensk "nurse" nu. Hun kom for 3 uker siden. Lillebror er snill om nettene igjen nu. Tro han sov formegit om dagen her en stunn.

12te.

Lillebror veier   Her sner igjen idag. Var kolt inat 11% snø er der bare 5 %oc.

15de

Prinsen reiste sig op alene i kurven sin idag for 1ste gang; men nu er han snart 10 mimeder

16de

Idag har lillebror fåt sin 8de tann. Han er sund og frisk maven har helt fra han var nyfødt virket 2 à 3 gange dag-lig og det gjør den fremdeles.

December 1937.

Hans daglige brod bestå r e av : 1 banan 3 kavringer 4 te seer semuljegryn 600 gr. melk. Sa, fen av 1½ appelsin, pureer av : ' uleiotter goteter, blomkål og spir et. Eplemos rödgröt, plommer, per -, kjott og fiskeboller som han be med 9 mnd. gammel. 2 teeskeer raw. råbringbar saft; av og til litt kalvebuljong.

26de.

Prins Harald v ier idag 8635 gr. Julaften ra - vi på Slottet og drak the mea kongen og dron- ningen. -g fik et lite sölvfat av hend a majestet.

Januar 9 de 1938.

Prins n veier idag 8915 gr. Har er sund + frisk og står ut - på verandaen i optil 9 % kulde og er varm + god når jeg tar ham inn. Her

December, 1937

[16th Cont.] His daily diet now consists of a banana, three rusks, four teaspoons of semolina, 600 grams milk, the juice from one and a half oranges, purées *of carrots, potatoes, cauli- flower, and spinach,. When he was nine months old he also began eating applesauce, plums, pears, meat, and fish balls. In addition to this, he gets two teaspoons of cod liver oil, raw raspberry juice, and sometimes a little "kalvebuljong" (veal-based bouillon).*

[Inga's Christmas at Skaugum, December 26]

26th

Prince Harald weighs 8,635 grams today. On Christmas Eve, we went to the palace, and had tea with the King and the Queen. Her Highness gave me a small silver platter.

January 9, 1938

Lillebror weighs 8,915 grams now. He's healthy as always and likes to be outside, even in minus 9 degrees [about +16°F]. When I bring him back inside he is warm and com- fortable. [Cont.]

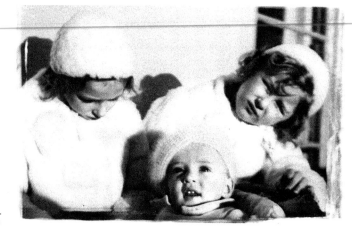

The two sisters were dressed like their brother, all three wearing fashionable white *berets*.

A Norwegian elkhound pulled the Prince along the newly-plowed roads.

[Newspaper Article]

*Prince Harald is one year old today, and has
posed for the photographer for this occasion.
We show here in the photograph his Royal
Highness in the playroom at Skaugum, where
the Prince rules the roost while the Princesses
are being tutored. Prince Harald is big and
healthy and very advanced for his age. At the
moment he is an expert at crawling. When he
supports himself on the playpen he can walk a
few steps as well, and when his sisters, Astrid
or Ragnhild are allowed to hold his arms he
stands up like a grownup. It won't be long
before he takes his first steps by himself. He
has blond, curly hair, eight shining white teeth,
and speaks a language that, for the time being,
only those closest to him can understand. He is
a charming little fellow, say those who have
seen him, and don't the pictures of him verify
this?*

*The big day will be celebrated quietly at
Skaugum, since the Prince is too young to have
a children's party. But the Crown Prince cou-
ple will arrive in town this afternoon.
[Probably from Tidens Tegn, circa
February 28, 1938]*

Arveprins **Harald** er 1 år idag, og
har i den anledning posert for foto-
grafen. Vi presenterer hans kongelige
høihet i lekestuen på Skaugum, hvor
arveprinsen er enehersker de timer
prinsessene opholder sig i skolestuen.
Prins Harald er stor og frisk og langt
fremme for sin alder. Han er for øie-
bikket ekspert i kryping og krabbing,
han går når han holder sig i lekegrinden og strekker sig som en voksen kar,
når søster Astrid eller søster Ragnhild
får lov til å holde i armene. Det va-
rer ikke lenge, før han tar de første
selvstendige skritt på livets vei. Han
har blondt hår som krøller sig
i nakken, åtte skinnende, hvite tenner og snakker et sprog som bare de
innviede foreløbig skjønner noget av.
Han er i alle deler en inntagende liten
plugg, sier de som har sett ham, og gir
kanskje ikke billedene arveprinsens
utallige beundrere rett?

Dagen vil bli feiret i all stillhet på
Skaugum, arveprinsen er for liten til å
ha barneselskap. Men kronprinsparet
kommer i løpet av formiddagen til by-

Harald held up a large rattle,
one of his birthday gifts.

The jeweler, Tostrup, crafted the 12 silver plates and took
these close-up photographs of them as well as of a specially
made mahogany chest to hold the plates.

Januar 1938.

er stor sne og den sner stadig
fin, fint føre; men nu blir
det nok mildvær. Den 16de 9000 gr.

23de
Prinsen veier 9040 gr. han vokser
og legger på sig hver uke
men ikke så meget nu længer
bare 40 gr. denne uke; men så
har han 4 netter efter hverandre
skreket og vært urolig så jeg
trodde sikkert at han hadde
fåt meslinger som prinsesse
Ragnhild har fåtiden; men
siste nat sov han helt rolig
igjen og om dagen er han
i godt humør. Både forrige
uke og denne har det vært mild
vær og delvis regn idag 10 varmegr.
og skålende sol. Sneen er skrumpet
betydelig inn.

30de
Prinsen veier idag 9230 gr.
Skålende sol! Milt og fint skiføre.
Mysne. Jeg var uk på ski med prinsessene

Februar 1938.

10de
Lillebror veier 9270 gr. han
er hver dag i full vigør og ser
uk for å trives rigtig godt.
Både igår og idag er her stort
selskap. Igår 33 og idag 49 gjester.
Jeg var idag uk med prinsessene
på ski, fint føre men hårdt
og glat.

14de
Prins Harald har samme
vegt idag. Igår var her 42
barn + voksne i Astrids gebursdag
Prinsen var ikke nede; damene
kom op og hilste på ham.

21de
Han er et år idag og
veier 9480 gr. Her er intet selskap idag. Kongen og dronningen
var her til lunch og te, og han
fik sine både store + små
gaver, mest leker, men og
en pengegave fra K.N.S som
grunnfond til hytte på Hankø.

January, 1938

*[9th Cont.] The snow keeps coming down—
great for skiing but I'm sure it will be mild
again soon. The 16th: 9,000 grams.*

23rd
*The Prince is still growing and gaining weight
every week—he now weighs 9,040 grams—
but he's not growing as fast anymore, only 40
grams this week. Then again, he's been restless
and crying these past 4 nights, and I was almost
convinced he'd caught the measles[54] from Princess
Ragnhild, but last night he slept well again, and
he was in a good mood during the day. Both
last week and this week we've had mild weather
and some rain. Today it's 10 degrees [48°F]
and sunny. The snow is quickly melting away.*

30th
*The Prince weighs 9,230 grams today. Sunny
weather and nice new snow for skiing. I went
skiing with the Princesses.*

[54] Measles is an acute, infectious, communicable viral disease
of young children characterized by small red spots on the
skin, high fever and nasal discharge.

[One-Year Birthday of Prince Harald]

February, 1938

10th
Lillebror *weighs 9,270 grams. He is full of
energy and seems to be thriving. There were
big parties here both yesterday and today—
33 guests yesterday and 49 today. I was out
skiing with the Princesses today; the snow was
nice, but hard and slippery.*

14th
*Prince Harald weighs the same today. Yesterday,
we had 42 children and adults here for Astrid's
birthday party.[55] The Prince didn't attend the
party. The ladies came upstairs to see him.*

21st
*Harald is one year old today, and weighs
9,480 grams. There was no birthday party,
but the King and Queen came for lunch, and
stayed for tea as well.* Lillebror *received
many presents, both large and small, mostly
toys, but also a gift of money from KNS,
towards a cabin at Hankø.[56]*

[55] Princess Astrid was born on February 12, 1932, making this
her sixth birthday.

[56] KNS is an abbreviation for the Royal Yacht Association
(*Kongelig Norsk Seilforening*). The island of Hankø is known
for its yacht club and international boat racing

[Newspaper Article]

… at 12:30 P.M. at the Royal Palace, they will receive the one-year gift from the women of Norway.

As mentioned last Saturday, the National Council[57] has received many donations from all across the country over the years. The money was supposed to go towards the Prince's baptismal gift, but the money arrived too late. Therefore, this money has been put towards a new gift, a plate and a fork in pure gold. This gift also matches the porridge spoon, the milk glass, and the spoon that the women of Norway gave the Prince earlier. It has the same ornaments, the same warm and light gold, the same luster, and the same initials. The gift was in a red leather box lined with white velvet, and has the Prince's monogram on the cover. It's a simple and beautiful gift, worthy of a royal birthday boy. As an interesting aside, the fork was the first gold fork ever to be made at Tostrup *jewelers.[58]*

[Probably Tidens Tegn, *circa February 28, 1938.]*

[57]The National Council of Norwegian Women (*Norske Kvinners Nasjonalråd*) is a philanthropic organization with headquarters in Oslo.

[58]*Tostrup* is a well-established jewelry store in Oslo, located on Karl Johans Gate, specializing in silver gift items.

en, hvor de klokken 12.30 på slottet vil motta 1-års gaven fra de norske kvinner.

— — —

Som vi nevnte lørdag har Nasjonalrådet i årets løp stadig fått småbeløp fra forskjellige kanter av landet. Pengene var ment som et bidrag til arveprinsens dåpsgave fra de norske kvinner, men kom for sent. og for restsummen har Norske Kvinners Nasjonalråd bestilt en ny gave, bestående av en tallerken og en gaffel i rent gull. Gaven står helt i stil med grøttallerkenen, melkekruset og skjeen som var arveprinsens dåpsgave fra de norske kvinner. Den har samme ornamentikk, samme varme, lyse gulltone, samme glans og samme navnetrekk. Gaven ligger i et rødt skinnetui foret med hvit fløiel, og har arveprinsens monogram på lokket. Det er en enkel og nydelig gave, verdig et kongelig geburtsdagsbarn, og som et kuriosum kan vi nevne at arveprinsens gaffel er den første gullgaffel som har vært laget i Tostrups verksted.

Playing in the freshly fallen snow, Prince Harald proudly shows off his new coat, made of Norwegian reindeer skin.

Prince Harald was on the Red Cross stamp for five years to raise money for the organization.

Februar 1938.
27de Vekt 9580. Han er lei
grøten sin nu & skriker når han
skal spise den. Kronprinsparret er
i Stockholm i prins Carls geburtsdag.
1ste Mars
På Skaugum har vi nu haft
tyk tåke i 5 dage, men lysnet
idag, det var rent rart å se
sjøen igjen. Tåken har vært så
tyk ut den har ligget helt inn
på huset. Lillebror har allikevel
vært ute om formiddagen.
Han forsøker å spise smabrød nu
og havregröt får han ogsa.
5te Prins Harald reiste sig op
og stod i lekegrinden sin for
första gang igår. På 1årsdagen
kunne han "bake kake!
Et par uker för kunne
han vise "hvor stor" han var
6te. Holmenkolldagen. Lillebror

February, 1938

27th

Weight: 9,580 grams. He's tired of porridge now and cries when he gets it. The Crown Prince couple is in Stockholm for Prince Carl's birthday.

March, 1938

1st

We've had thick fog at Skaugum for five days now, but it finally went away today, and it was strange to be able to see the fjord again. The fog was so thick it lay right up to the house, but Lillebror was outside in the afternoon anyway. He tries to eat sandwiches now, and I'm feeding him oatmeal, too.

5th

Prince Harald stood by himself for the first time yesterday. At his first birthday, he knew how to "pat-a-cake" too. A couple of weeks before that, he knew how to show "how big" he was.

6th

"Holmenkolldagen."[59] Lillebror *[Cont.]*

[59]Holmenkollen Day (*Holmenkolldagen*) and ski festival make up the oldest organized skiing event in the world, with over one million people attending each year during the 11 days in March.

Queen Maud took a photo of three generations of skiers.

The rolling terrain and dry snow at Sikkilsdalen made the lodge an ideal cross-country ski retreat.

March, 1938

[6th Cont.] and I are home alone. The others are at the ski hill [Holmenkollen ski jump].

20th

Today, his ninth tooth broke through, and soon the tenth one will be visible too. He can sit up by himself in the playpen now. We have beautiful weather and the snow is melting quickly. The Crown Prince couple is at Gausdal[60] this week; the Princesses are gone for tea, and the Prince and I are home alone today.

April, 1938

12th

The Crown Prince couple left on their Easter trip this Saturday. Prince Harald has 10 teeth and he's growing nicely. He stopped taking cod-liver oil on April 1. Olga Olsen[61] [from Bagn and a friend of Marie and Inga] was here yesterday, and took pictures of the Princesses, the Prince, and me.

[60]Gausdal *(Sikkilsdalen)* is in a valley in the *Jotunheimen* Range, about 180 miles northwest of Oslo, where the Royal Family has a mountain chalet, *Prinsehytta*, given to Crown Prince Olav by Prince Gustav of Sweden.

[61]Olga Olsen was from Bagn, Inga's home town, and was friend of Inga. She was a professional photographer working in Oslo.

The Prince was an avid cross-country skier and, likewise, a builder of snowmen.

April, 1938

April 1938.

Hele april har vært vått surt & kalt ikke regn. Prins Harald han veide den 27de april 10200 gr. så det er en fin forøkelse. Han får fremdeles bananer + kavringgrøt til morgenmat, men nu smør brød til frokost. Ellers kjøtt + fiskeboller, av & til rått ska- let kjøt, kylling, kalvekjøtt & de forskjellige grønsaker.

Mai

16de
Harald spiste idag for førske gang brødet sit med skorpe på og det gik fint. Han fik 1 helt stykke med gjetost 1/2 med marmolade. Han er nu så glad i smørbrød likedan i middagsmat grøter er han lit lei nu.

April, 1938

All of April has been cold and nasty and without rain. Prince Harald weighed 10,200 grams on March 27, so he's gaining weight nicely. He still gets bananas and rusks for his first meal of the day, but now eats sandwiches for breakfast. He's also getting a lot of meat-balls and fishballs, now and then chicken, veal, raw meat finely minced, and various vegetables.

May, 1938

<u>16th</u>
Today for the first time Harald ate his bread with the crust on, and it went fine. He ate one whole slice with goat cheese and another half slice with jam. He loves sandwiches and meat and potatoes. He is tired of porridge now.

Harald's horse was called *Moro* .

Crown Prince Olav and Prince Harald at the helm of their sailing boat.

Harald with the family dog called *Vimse*.

May, 1938

17th

We left at 9:30 this morning and arrived at the Palace at 10:00 A.M. However, the Children's Parade was extremely delayed and did not show up until 10:40 A.M. Prince Harald was out on the balcony until 11:00 A.M., when I brought him inside to feed him. The Crown Princess held him in her arms the whole time. The Crown Prince couple and the children ate at the palace, but I brought the Prince home. Lillebror was on his best behavior.

June, 1938

9th

We were all gathered at Bygdøy Kongsgård for Princess Ragnhild's birthday.[62] Russen [graduating seniors][63] came and gave her a present, as in previous years. A large pearl on a gold necklace. The Russen president gave a speech in her honor and called her the fairest flower among the young women of Norway, one everyone looks up to. [Cont.]

[62]Ragnhild was born on June 4, 1930 and was celebrating her 8th birthday.

[63]*Russen* refers to members of the graduating class of a *gymnasium*. During the last four months of the school year, many special events take place.

The two sisters took their brother out for a bicycle/tricycle ride on the gravel roads around the mansion.

From the family telescope Harald viewed the boats on the Oslo Fjord.

His small car was powered by his feet.

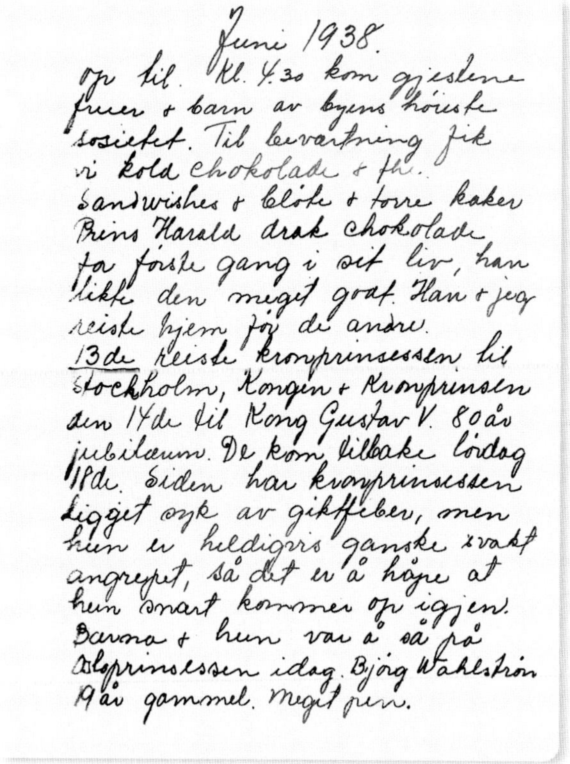

Juni 1938.

[Handwritten Norwegian, top left:]

op til. Kl. 4.30 kom gjestene fruer + barn av byens höieste sosietet. Til bevertning fik vi kold chokolade + th. Sandwishes + chløh + tørre kaker Prins Harald drak chokolade for förste gang i sit liv, han likte den meget godt. Han + jeg reiste hjem för de andre.

13de Reiste kronprinsessen til Stockholm, Kongen + Kronprinsen den 14de til Kong Gustav V. 80 års jubileum. De kom tilbake lördag 18de. Siden har kronprinsessen ligget syk av giktfeber, men hun er heldigvis ganske svakt angrepet, så det er å håpe at hun snart kommer op igjen. Barna + hun var å så på Osloprinsessen idag. Björg Wahlström 19 år gammel. Meget pen.

[Handwritten Norwegian, bottom left:]

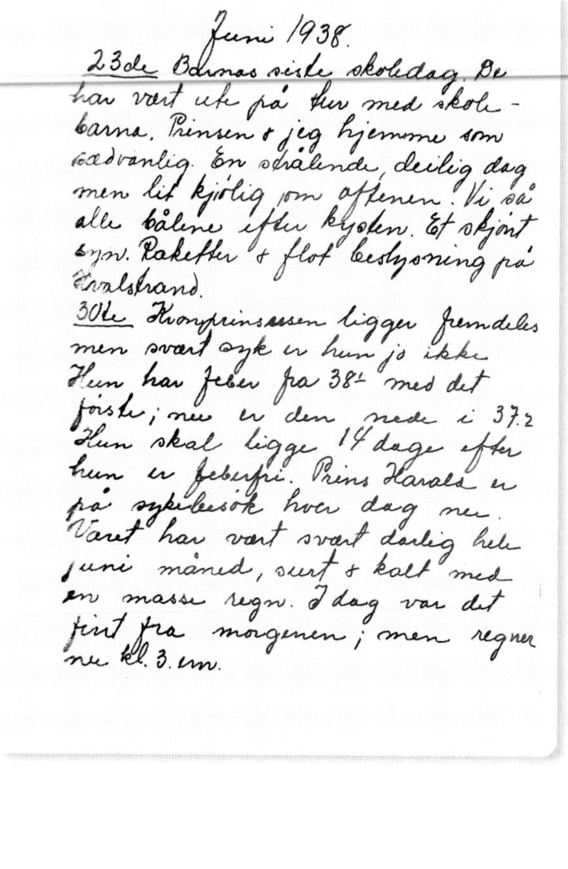

Juni 1938.

23de Barnas siste skoledag. De har vært ute på tur med skolebarna. Prinsen + jeg hjemme som sædvanlig. En strålende, deilig dag men lit kjölig om aftenen. Vi så alle bålene efter kysten. Et skjönt syn. Raketter + flot belysning på Hvalstrand.

30te Kronprinsessen ligger fremdeles men svært syk er hun jo ikke. Hun har feber fra 38½ med det förste; nu er den nede i 37.2 Hun skal ligge 14 dage efter hun er feberfri. Prins Harald er på sykebesök hver dag nu. Været har vært svært dårlig hele juni måned, surt + kalt med en masse regn. Idag var det fint fra morgenen; men regner nu kl. 3. em.

June, 1938

[9th Cont.] At 4:30 P.M., the guests arrived–women and children from the highest social rank of the city. We were served chocolate milk and tea, sandwiches, and several types of cakes and cookies. Prince Harald had chocolate milk for the first time in his life; he liked it a lot. We went home a while before the others.

13th

The Crown Princess went to Stockholm on the 13th, and the King on the 14th, to attend King Gustav's 80th birthday celebration. They returned on Saturday the 18th. Since then, the Crown Princess has been sick with "giktfeber."[64] Luckily, it hasn't hit her too hard, so she'll hopefully be up and feeling better soon.

She and the children went to see the "Oslo Princess Today". Bjørg Wahlstrøm, 19 years old, [was chosen and was] very pretty.[65]

[64] *Giktfeber* is rheumatic fever. The symptoms are chronic inflammation of joints, fever along with pain and swelling of the joints.

[65] Beginning in 1933 Oslo Day (*Oslodagen*) was initiated by the Director (*Turistsjef*) of the Oslo Tourist Board, Alfhild Hovdan.

June, 1938

23rd

The last day of school for the children. They went on a field trip, the Prince and I were at home as usual. A beautiful day, but a little colder towards the afternoon. We saw the bonfires along the coast at night. A beautiful sight. Fireworks and beautiful lighting from Hvalstrand.[66]

30th

The Crown Princess is still in bed but fortunately is not very ill. She had a 38.5-degree about 101.3°F] fever, now it's down to 37.2 degrees [about 99°F]. She's supposed to stay in bed for another 14 days after the fever is gone. Prince Harald visits her every day. The weather has been pretty poor all of June, lots of rain and nasty weather. This morning started out nice, but it's been raining in the afternoon.

[66] Hvalstrand is a small community on the *Oslofjorden*. There, and all over Norway, bonfires are lit on Midsummer Night to celebrate the summer solstice.

July, 1938

7th

Nasty weather and strong wind. Prince Harald got a fever three days ago; the first night he was so sick I had to stay up with him half the night. He's better now, and his fever is reduced from 37.7 degrees [about 100°F] and 38.8 degrees [about 102°F)] to 37.3 degrees [about 99°F]. Hope he'll be well by tomorrow morning. This is the first time he's been ill since I've been with him. I had hoped he would stay healthy for my entire stay here, but that's not the way it turned out. The Crown Princess [Märtha] is still ill, and Princess Ingeborg [her mother] keeps her company most of the time, which is nice. But since the Crown Princess is not very ill, I am sure that they have a nice time together. Harald weighs 10,920 grams now.

July, 1938

12th

Prince Harald has had rubella.[67] The rash came the third day, but by then the fever had passed. He's stayed inside for a week, and was outside for the first time on Tuesday afternoon. He looks a little pale.

19th

Lots of rain in July too, but yesterday was gorgeous sunshine. We went out to the rose garden, which looks beautiful now after all the rain, and took pictures of Harald and Astrid. Harald looks better now, and has gotten tan despite the gray weather. It rained for a little bit today too, but now the sun is peeking out again.

22nd

Prince Harald was down by [Cont.]

67 Rubella, called German measles in the United States, occurs most often in children and is characterized by small red spots on the skin, high fever and nasal discharge.

Juli 1938.

7de Surt + kaldt vær og en svær vind. Prins Harald har fåt feber for 3 dage siden; den første nat var han riktig dårlig + jeg gik oppe med ham halve natten. Siden er han bedre + temperaturen som var 37,7 m. og 38,8 a. er nu nede i 37,3. iaften så håper nu at han er bra igjen til imorgen. Det er første gang han er syk i den tiden jo. har været her. Jeg hadde håpet at han skulle holdt sig frisk den tiden jeg var her; men slik gik det altså ikke. Kronprinsessen er syk fremdeles. Prinsesse Ingeborg er her og holder henne med selskap. K. er jo ikke meget syk så de har det nok hyggeligt sammen. Han veier 10920 gr. nu.

Juli 1938.

12te Prins Harald har hat røde hunde. Utslettet kom 3die dag; men han var da helt uten temperatur. Han var i det hele inne en uke og var ute for første gang igjen tirsdag em. Han er blit litt blek.

19de. Masse regn i Juli ogsaa; men igår en strålende solskin vi var ute i rosenhaven som er vidunderlig vakker nu efter alt regnet og tok noen bilder av Harald + Astrid. Harald ser godt ut igjen nu + er blit brun tiltrods for gråværet. Det har regnet idag også; men nu titter solen frem.

22de Prins Harald var nede ved

Juli 1938

Badehuset i Vallen + badet i sjøvann for første gang onsdag den 19 juli. Han likte + vasse; men da det kolde sjøvann kom på kroppen skrek han + vilde op igjen. Vannet var 20°. Dagen efter gik det bedre da fik han vann på hele sig.

27de Prins Harald har vært dårlig inat. Han har ingen feber, men han kastet op både igår + i nat Idag er han bra; men har ingen matlyst.

28de Lillebror hadde feber i 38° igåraftes. Han har vært riktig urolig inat + hadde 38.2 idag. Han har ikke kastet op senere. men han har nok hat mavesmerte. I em. er han roligere. Så er han vel bra igjen imorgen.

July, 1938

[22nd Cont.] the beach house at Vollen[68] and went swimming in the fjord for the first time on Wednesday July 19. He liked wading, but when the cold salt water covered his body, he started screaming and wanted to be picked up. The water was 20 degrees [about 68°F]. The day after it went better and he let the water cover his whole body.

27th

Prince Harald was sick last night. He doesn't have a fever, but he's been vomiting for two days. Today he's feeling better, but was not hungry.

28th

Lillebror had a fever of 38 degrees [about 100.4°F] last evening. He's been very restless all night, and had a 38.2-degree [about 101°F] fever today. He has not been vomiting, but I think his stomach hurts. Since he's better this afternoon, I hope he'll be all well tomorrow.

[68] Vollen is located on the *Oslofjorden* on the beach below Skaugum. The Royal Family had a beach house for changing clothes. Vollen was the home of author Nini Roll Anker and her husband Johan who was an engineer and boat builder. Johan built boats for the Royal Family and the Royal Family beach house was on his property.

[Inga Leaves Skaugum, July 28, 1938]

School vacation meant many outdoor activities for the two sisters who often hid from their brother in their tent.

The Prince played on the swings.

Epilogue
The Continuing Lives of Prince Harald and Inga Berg

Prince Harald led a parade of his fellow students on **Syttende Mai** *in 1944 at Pook's Hill White Hall Country School, Bethesda, Maryland, where he was a pupil.*

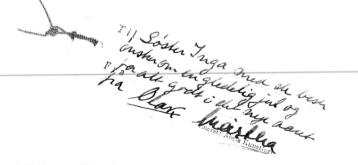

The epilogue continues the stories of Prince Harald and Inga Berg and their families following Inga's service at Skaugum, through the trying times of World War II and up to the present. Prince Harald was consecrated King Harald V in 1991. Inga Berg continued her nursing career until her retirement, remaining in communication with the Royal Family.

Conclusion of Inga's Service at Skaugum

On July 30, 1938, after 18 months of caring for Prince Harald, Inga left service at the Crown Prince residence for her next home nursing position in the Oslo area. It was a common practice among well-to-do Norwegians to hire pediatric nurses to care for infants during their first two very vulnerable years. After that parents often switched to tutors for music, sports or language study. After Inga's service, a regular nurse as well as a physician remained on staff at Skaugum to meet the Royal Family's medical needs. It was clear that the Crown Prince and Princess

A Christmas gift card was signed personally by Crown Prince Olav and Crown Princess Märtha reading: "To Sister Inga Berg with best wishes and a Merry Christmas with all the best for the New Year." [Note: At this time in Norway nurses were often referred to as "sisters" as a sign of respect but with no religious connotations.

were pleased with Inga's tenure in their home because they maintained contact and cordially included her in Harald's milestone celebrations.

PASSING OF QUEEN MAUD

Just two months after Inga completed her service, the Royal Family suffered a blow. While on her annual autumn visit to her native England, Queen Maud took ill. She died on November 20, 1938, six days before her 69th birthday. The loss of the Queen weighed especially heavily on King Haakon and Crown Prince Olav because when the three of them came to Norway in 1905 as foreigners in a new land they remained somewhat insulated as a family, and dependent on each other for personal counsel and support.

In the war years that were almost upon them, the remaining Royals would need counsel and support such as they never had before. Haakon never remarried. Crown Princess Märtha stepped up to represent the Monarchy in many ways, and also to become an even closer friend and great comfort to the King. The Crown Prince increasingly shared the King's burdens of duty.[24]

Queen Maud's public shyness and inability to speak the Norwegian language had given many Norwegians a negative opinion, but within her circle of family and friends she was remembered as lively and vital. Observations by Inga, who could converse easily in English with the Queen, were quite favorable: "Queen Maud, who is a kind and good-natured person, is completely taken with Prince Harald; she can play with him for hours…Both the King and Queen have been so friendly lately. They have played with Harald every afternoon for about an hour." Inga recalled: "What I remember the most is a Christmas Eve in the castle, in 1937. I had Queen Maud and Crown Princess Märtha by my side during the dinner, [Inga was holding 10 month old Prince Harald on her lap] with the rest of the Royal Family around us. This was a big moment to me. The Queen was very sweet."[25]

The lasting image of Queen Maud paled in comparison to those who survived her because she died just short of what would be the modern defining period of the Norwegian Monarchy and of all Norway, World War II. In the story of Inga Berg and Prince Harald, all of the characters who experienced the war years were severely tested.

GERMAN INVASION APRIL 9, 1940

The relatively carefree days at Skaugum that characterized the first three years of the new Prince's life came to an abrupt end in April of 1940, six weeks after Harald's third birthday. Norway had been maintaining nervous neutrality between warring European powers Germany and Great Britain, and was belatedly planning to bolster defenses. Meanwhile almost the entire German fleet, plus 60,000 troops and the *Luftwaffe* (air force), were secretly positioned to implement a simultaneous invasion at seven strategic points from Oslo around to the town of Narvik on the far northern coast. German forces were also prepared to invade Denmark, which was to serve as a strategic airbase for sorties over Norway and the North Sea.[26]

The operation, code named *Weserübung,* (Wesar River exercise) commenced at 4:15 A.M. on April 9. In *blitzkrieg* mode the German forces were rapidly successful against the poorly prepared Danes and against the Norwegian defenses at Narvik, Trondheim, Bergen, Egersund, Kristiansand, and Arendal; but the Germans were impeded on their approach to Oslo. The largest of the German invading forces was detected passing through the entrance to the *Oslofjord.* Thirty miles into the fjord and ten miles south of the capital, it proceeded under cover of darkness

Nazi Germany invaded Norway on April 9, 1940 and for the first time in the history of warfare they used the tactic of combining forces of air, sea and land in one concerted attack.

into the Drøbak Narrows. From the vicinity of the Oscarsborg Fortress the Norwegians shelled the German fleet with antique 280 mm guns affectionately called Moses and Aaron, and from a concealed shore battery the Norwegians launched torpedoes that struck and sank the lead German ship, the heavy cruiser *Blücher*. The remaining ships turned south to offload troops and equipment for a time-consuming ground assault to neutralize the fortifications that defended the routes to Oslo.

INVASION DELAYED - EVACUATION FROM SKAUGUM AND OSLO

In an April 2 memo to invasion commanders, Adolf Hitler had stressed that at all costs the Norwegian King and government should be prevented from escape. Instead, thanks to the delay caused by the *Blücher's* demise and to quick thinking by *Storting* President Carl Joachim Hambro, King Haakon, the Royal Family, the State Council and most of the *Storting* were successfully evacuated by special train to the town of Hamar, about 60 miles north of the capitol. Officials were also able to remove the national gold reserves from the Bank of Norway and carry them north to be eventually shipped to the United States for safekeeping. Meeting at Hamar on April 9, and then later that day in the nearby town of Elverum, the Storting granted members of the State Council the legislative power to govern in exile, if necessary, for the duration of the war. This was called *Elverumsfullmakten* (the Elverum Authorization). Norwegian authorities informed U.S Embassy officials "that Norway considered herself at war with Germany."[27]

GERMANS CAPTURE THE CAPITAL

The German invaders augmented their aborted naval advance on Oslo with a daring airborne assault, the first such operation in the history of warfare. Paratroopers captured Fornebu Airfield and, with additional troops arriving on transport planes, marched into Oslo and secured it by noon on April 9, only a few hours after the Royal Family's train had departed for Hamar. Home forces, although unprepared to defend the capital, were able to slow the German advance in their attempt to establish supply routes to other coastal footholds. At the *Midtskogen* farm, three miles from Elverum, where Haakon and government officials were meeting, Royal Norwegian Guards and local volunteers defeated a crack unit of one hundred German troops which, after landing in Oslo, had been quickly dispatched north in an attempt to capture the King. The German naval convoy did not arrive in Oslo until midday on April 10.[28]

Nazi German soldiers marched down Karl Johans Gate in Oslo with the Royal Palace in the background and Oslo University on the right.

GERMAN PUPPET GOVERNMENT

On the first day of the invasion Vidkun Quisling of the *Nasjonal Samling* (NS or National Unity Party), declared himself the leader of a new government and ordered Norwegians to end resistance. Quisling had visited Hitler in Berlin a year earlier and had actually suggested the invasion. He was soon to be denounced by the King, ignored by the Norwegian people,

and therefore forced by the Germans to resign within a week. Germans set up a series of government front organizations, and eventually allowed Quisling to pose as Minister President. The real overall civilian authority was Josef Terboven, a ruthless German Nazi party operative who was appointed *Reichskommissar* (State's Commissar) by Hitler on April 24, and who set up headquarters in *Stortinget* (the parliament office buildings).

Vidkun Quisling reviewed Norwegian troops who had joined the Nazi German army and recently returned from battlefield operations in Europe, circa 1943.

Under his direction all political parties except the NS, were banned and labor organizations and local governments were forced to accept leaders only from that party. In September Josef Terboven established his personal residence at Skaugum.

Royal Family Separated

Upon arrival in Elverum it was already clear to Crown Prince Olav that his wife and children were being exposed to too much danger while traveling with the government contingent. Crown Princess Märtha, Prince Harald and Princesses Ragnhild and Astrid were rushed by motorcar to the Swedish border. At the border, according to an account by Princess Astrid, who was eight years old at the time, the Swedish border guards at first denied access for Märtha's party, but acquiesced when the Norwegian driver threatened to crash the gate. The contingent went first to *Høyfjellshotellet* in the mountain village of Sälen where they remained for two weeks. Then they relocated to the estate of Märtha's brother, Carl Bernadotte, at Fridhem near Stockholm. In Sweden the reception was chilly and their position precarious. Märtha's presence was not officially sanctioned; therefore she kept a very low profile and moved within Sweden quite often.

Prior to April 9 Sweden and Norway had both sought to remain neutral in the war between Germany and Great Britain. Sweden was coveted by the Germans for its iron ore and Norway for its fjords that offered year-round shelter from which the German navy could prey on the Atlantic shipping lanes. Adolf Hitler also feared that Norway, if not secured, might become a platform for an Allied counter-invasion of Europe, and conversely saw it as his first stepping stone for a German invasion of North America. The Germans saw invasion as their best way to deal with Norway, but chose to retain a peaceful trading relationship with agreeable, and significantly better armed, Sweden. In order to remain autonomous the Swedes cooperated as needed, including eventually allowing Germany to service its occupation of Norway by transporting troops and supplies across Sweden. In public opinion within Sweden, as within Norway, there was sympathy both for and against Germany.

THE ULTIMATUM

The German invasion was soon on firm footing. On April 10 the German envoy, Dr. Curt Bräuer met King Haakon at Elverum and, for the second time, demanded Norwegian capitulation. The Nazis wanted the King to endorse a new government headed by Quisling. Haakon relayed the Nazi demands, and his opinion of them, to the council. One translated account of his words: "I am deeply affected by the responsibility laid on me if the German demand is rejected. The responsibility for the calamities that will befall people and country is indeed so grave that I dread to take it. It rests with the government to decide, but my position is clear. For my part I cannot accept the German demands. It would conflict with all that I have considered to be my duty as King of Norway since I came to this country nearly thirty-five years ago." He went on to say that if the council decided to acquiesce he would abdicate rather than stand in their way.

The government weighed the consequences to which the King alluded and then unanimously agreed to reject the German ultimatum. The Norwegian government would strive to remain out from under the German jackboot in order to direct resistance, conduct international affairs, broadcast messages of hope to the people, and preserve the legitimacy of the 1814 Eidsvold Constitution.[29]

PURSUIT ACROSS NORWAY

After Dr. Bräuer relayed the final rejection of the ultimatum to Berlin, German aircraft fire-bombed Elverum. Olav and King Haakon saw the smoke from their hotel in nearby Nybergsund, and fled to the woods when the bombers turned their attention to that town. It was a drill that became very familiar in the next several weeks as the Germans used airplanes and spies to stalk the government party on its circuitous route by motorcar and train across southern Norway. Repeated attempts were mounted, using bombs or their paratroopers, to take Haakon and Olav "dead or alive," as they tried to reach a Norwegian army stronghold. They were denied temporary asylum in Sweden.

Meanwhile, the British Royal Navy destroyed the German fleet that had landed the invasion. On April 13 British troops came ashore near Narvik, and on April 17 they landed at Åndalsnes to join the Norwegian forces planning to retake Trondheim. The King's contingent completed a harrowing trek across Norway and arrived at the port of Molde on April 23. Molde was bombed almost continuously for the next six days, during which the allied prospects to retake Trondheim became hopeless. Southern Norway was lost. On April 29 the King, Crown Prince and the government boarded the British cruiser HMS *Glasgow* and were transported on a wide route around the continuing battle at Narvik and on to Tromsø, Norway.[30]

Battle of Bagn in Valdres: World War II Comes to Inga Berg's Home Town

After the German forces secured the *Oslofjorden* on April 10 they began a northward fan-shaped advance from Oslo following the river valleys on all available roads. It was a priority for them to link inland supply routes to their otherwise isolated and vulnerable forces to the north in Trondheim and in Narvik.

On April 14 the Germans captured the crossroads town of Hønefoss and proceeded from there in a two-pronged northward advance into the Valdres Valley. The main force moved east of the Randsfjord toward Gjøvik, and a somewhat lighter force of about 2000 men proceeded up along the Begna River toward the Berg family's hometown of Bagn. Oddmund Berg, with his family, fled ahead of the Germans from their new home in Hønefoss back to Bagn.

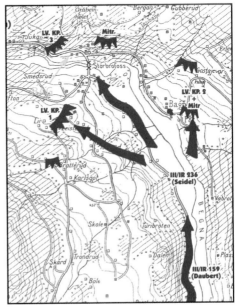

Arrows indicate the German army advance along the Begna River, April 18, 1940. The half crowns show the Norwegian defensive positions. The attack targeted the *Storebrofossen* bridge right next to Inga's house.

In Bagn, Oddmund's brother Ola Berg and his wife had a tailor shop and residence in the family house that had been built by Martin Berg on *Storebrofossen Plassen*. It is possible that Inga, who owned the nearby *Midtberg* building, was also in Bagn at that time.

Norwegian resistance built roadblocks and blew up bridges, while the local defense battalion of about 1000 men engaged the advancing Germans in delaying battles along the Begna River at the towns of Hen and Hallingby. After suffering heavy losses on April 16, the Norwegians fell back to prepare defensive positions in Bagn. The Germans initially valued the town for flank protection of the more direct routes to Trondheim.

Bagn was at a vital crossroads for German forces moving east from Voss, and was also on the main road to the Atlantic Ocean via the mighty *Sognefjorden*.

The Germans repaired bridges for troops as they proceeded up-river, but would need the *Storebrofossen* as the only substantial bridge north of Hønefoss on which their tanks could cross the Begna River from west to east on the main road. The Berg families and their neighbors evacuated their homes next to the bridge and fled to mountain farms like the Ellendshaugen farm of Inga's maternal grandparents.[31]

The Norwegians set up machine gun and rifle emplacements around the town of Bagn and its bridge, and at crossroads located to the south. The resistance forces threw dynamite onto the upstream ice in an attempt to cause the river to rise and prevent the Germans from crossing. When that failed, the Norwegian

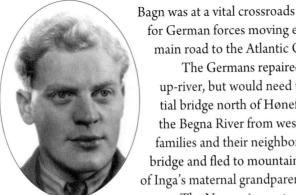

Arnfinn Rosenlund, 22 years old and a good friend of Arne Berg, was one of the two men who blew up the Bagn Bridge in order to stop the German advance.

75

resistance blew up the *Storebrofossen* bridge. On April 18 at 4:00 P.M., after skirmishes with Norwegian patrols south of town, the Germans approached Bagn from both sides of the river in a three-pronged attack. At 6:30 P.M. tanks from the primary German force on the main road arrived at the bridge area on the west side of the Begna, but of course could not cross, and withdrew under fire. At 10:00 P.M. they attempted a coordinated frontal attack. For a day and a half the Norwegians in Bagn held on all fronts, and on April 20 the Norwegians counterattacked and drove the main force of Germans sixty miles back down-river to Hønefoss. German soldiers attempting a flanking maneuver in the mountains above town were captured on April 21.[32]

The Bagn defenders took up new positions south of town and held against repeated attacks, but the poorly-armed home forces in the Valdres Valley were forced into a stalemate and then a retreat by the modern, mechanized German army. The Norwegian general in command agreed to a ceasefire, and then a formal capitulation on May 1. The Bagn defenders, who over 14 days of pitched battles had never retreated, disbanded and melted into the hills. German occupation forces entered Bagn and the German officers eventually used the former Fjellheim Hotel on the Plassen for quarters and offices.

KING HAAKON, CROWN PRINCE OLAV WITHDRAW TO ENGLAND

King Haakon, Crown Prince Olav, and the rest of the legitimate government did their best to represent Norway from Tromsø as Allied countries, with distractions all across Europe, scraped together military resources to attempt to counter the German invaders in Norway. On May 10 Germany invaded Belgium, the Netherlands, Luxembourg and France. An Allied force, which included Polish and French army troops, continued pressure at Narvik and retook it on May 28.

On June 3 Germany bombed Paris, France, and the struggle in Norway became a relatively minor concern for Britain and other Allies. By June 6, just nine days after establishing a foothold, the last foreign Allied force on Norwegian soil withdrew from Narvik. Before leaving they destroyed the rail and port facilities in order to delay Germany's further access to Swedish iron ore. On June 7, 1940, a last meeting of the Council of State took place at Tromsø, at which it was determined that the Norwegian home defense against Germany would officially end, and that the government would continue to operate from Great Britain.

The King and his only son had developed a close relationship, one that had strengthened after the death of Queen Maud. Haakon valued Olav as an advisor and confidant and included him when considering almost all of his important wartime decisions. At the last meeting in Tromsø the Crown Prince formally offered to remain in occupied Norway in order to intervene as he could on behalf of the state and the people. His noble proposal was respectfully declined, and that evening the King, Crown Prince and other officials boarded the British cruiser *Devonshire* which carried them to England.

Approximately 12 warships, 400 naval officers and enlisted men, and a few other service personnel from the army and air corps sailed with them to London. This group formed the staff of the Norwegian government in exile and the seed of a foreign-based Nordic fighting force. On June 10 the armed forces in Norway formally surrendered. On June 14 the German Army entered Paris and the world wondered how it could be stopped.

HAAKON'S RADIO BROADCASTS SUSTAIN HOPE IN NORWAY

In England, King Haakon was concerned that, as the occupation became more entrenched, the Norwegian people would abandon hope of a free Norway and would collaborate with the Germans. That fear was not unfounded, for the original Norwegian position had been neutrality, with invasion by either Germany or Britain seen as possibilities. Many Norwegians were bitterly disappointed in their government for not adequately defending the country.

King Haakon broadcasting one of his in-exile speeches to Norway from a BBC radio studio in 1940.

Some accepted the Germans' pretext to invasion that they were defending Norway from Britain. Others, like Quisling, were seduced by Nazi theory that held Nordic characteristics as ideal in their "Master Race."

In fact, about ten percent of the Norwegian population favored the German occupiers and 5,000 volunteered to serve in the German army, many in the SS. But the number of collaborators remained relatively low. One significant reason was that King Haakon made the Norwegian people aware, by BBC radio broadcast, of the efforts of the Allies and of Norwegians to defeat Germany and liberate Norway. Though oppressed, Norwegians took pride in their leaders, armed forces, merchant marine, and the Norwegian resistance.

On July 8, 1940 King Haakon made his first radio broadcast from London to Norway. In it he flatly rejected the advice that he had received from many quarters: to abdicate in order to appease the occupiers. He cited his duty as defined by the 1814 Constitution and underlined by the 1905 plebiscite of the people. In that, and in many broadcasts to follow, the King rallied the support of the people in Norway and, as spokesman for the Resistance, strengthened his leadership image.

King Haakon stated on August 27, 1940, "I think we did right… [to choose] that side which stands for the right of small nations to lead their own lives." The speeches also made the nature of Norway's struggle more apparent to foreign governments and to expatriate Norwegians.[33]

CROWN PRINCESS MÄRTHA AND CHILDREN EVACUATED TO THE U.S.

After the King and Crown Prince left Norwegian soil for England, they recognized that the situation in Sweden for the Crown Princess and children was becoming significantly more difficult. Minister of Justice Karl Gustaf Westman was one of several Swedish politicians who wanted the Norwegian Royals returned to Oslo so that the Germans, declaring Haakon and Olav abdicators, could install the toddler Prince Harald as king regent. Westman may have enjoyed the ironic parallel to the 1905 deposition of Swedish King Oscar II as ruler of Norway because he lacked Norwegian representation.

Florence Jaffray Hurst Harriman was working in Sweden to extricate Märtha and the children. Harriman had been appointed by President Franklin Roosevelt in 1937 as American Minister to Norway. She had fled Oslo under German attack along with the Norwegian government and then, unable to follow the government to Tromsø and on to London, she had also sought refuge in Sweden.

On July 25 President Roosevelt ordered the converted cruise ship, the *American Legion*, to sail from New York to the small Finnish seaport of Petsamo near Murmansk, Soviet Union on the Barents Sea, with specific orders to transport the Crown Princess and her children to the United States. According to the American Secretary of State the ship would "likewise bring back to this country such Americans in Scandinavian countries as can be accommodated and as may not be able to return safely in any other way."

On April 30, 1939, Prince Olav and Princess Märtha had traveled to the World's Fair in New York City to dedicate a Norwegian exhibit. At that time they met Franklin and Eleanor Roosevelt and accepted an invitation to spend the weekend at Springwood, the Roosevelt retreat home outside of Washington, D.C. The visit is commemorated today by a photograph of the four hanging in the Dresden Room at Springwood. It was that contact and resulting friendship, a year before the war, which later moved President Roosevelt to personally offer Märtha and her family political asylum.

On August 12 Märtha's entourage left the Solna summer home of Swedish Crown Prince Gustav Adolf, near Stockholm. Their automobile and train journey took them across Sweden and then over portions of Finland and Russia scarred by the recently-ended winter war. They arrived at Petsamo on August 15 and boarded the *American Legion*, along with Minister Harriman and almost 900 American nationals and other refugees from a number of Northern European countries. They set sail on August 16 and arrived in New York under U.S. navy destroyer escort twelve days later.

The president of the Norwegian *Storting*, Carl Hambro, met Märtha, the children, and their party, and took them to the Waldorf Astoria Hotel. As soon as they arrived at the hotel, Märtha telephoned Crown Prince Olav in London. It had been more than five weeks since they had last been able to speak to each other.

Crown Princess Märtha with her three children arrived at the pier in New York City, August 28, 1940.

A U.S. HOME AT POOK'S HILL

President Roosevelt invited Märtha, together with her children and numerous staff members to once again stay at Springwood, at least until a suitable home could be found. With the help and influence of Roosevelt, the Norwegian government found a mansion in Bethesda, Maryland about four miles from the Norwegian Embassy, and purchased it for $222,000 borrowed from the gold reserves moved to the U. S. from Oslo on April 9. The name of the estate was Pook's Hill, taken from Rudyard Kipling's 1906 story, "Puck of Pook's Hill." Merle Thorp, the founder and publisher of *Nation's Business* magazine, had built it in 1927. After several months at Springwood, Princess Märtha and her children moved into the mansion.

Hjemmet (the home) was the name the Royal Family gave to the mansion where they resided during the five years of World War II. It was located just outside Washington, D.C. Astrid was taking the photograph of her family.

The Princesses Ragnhild and Astrid were enrolled in White Hall Country School, a little private school in the neighborhood, and Prince Harald began at the London Preschool which was also was nearby. In 1943 he joined his two sisters at White Hall. It was ironic that Olav and Märtha had provided infant Harald with a specifically Norwegian nurse, Inga Berg, to influence his first two years, but that international events dictated that his first formal education was in foreign schools. Reminders of Norway were, no doubt, maintained at Pook's Hill, and Harald's American exposure served him well in his later years.[34]

Inga's Life During the Occupation

After leaving the royal service at Skaugum, Inga continued to work with the Women's Clinic in Oslo and the Red Cross Hospital as well as responding to the many individual requests for her services. When not in a client's residence or with family in Bagn, Inga lived in downtown Oslo between the Royal Palace and Vigeland's Park at Prof Dahls Gate 19.

The Woman's Clinic in Oslo where Inga was trained and where she continued to work during the War.

The biggest problem for Inga and other nurses was that the Germans immediately confiscated all disinfectants and medical supplies. Nurses were forced to make bandages from all types of cloth and secretly hide these supplies in private homes to keep them away from the Gestapo. They were not allowed to wear their official pins on their uniforms. These pins pictured the sun breaking through the sky symbolizing their ideal of service to the Norwegian people. Nor were they permitted to use stationery or printed materials with their motto "Always Ready". The nurses used these words to indicate their willingness to continue the struggle against the occupation in spite of very challenging working conditions.

Daily life in Oslo from 1940 to 1945, and even after the war, was marked by severe shortages of food and supplies. Norway, with a low percentage of farm land, had always relied on fishing and importing, but during the war those activities all but stopped. Germany was the only trading partner and was in no position to share. Norwegians resorted to growing as much of their own food as possible, so Inga and others living in population centers like Oslo fared the worst.

A huge standing force of over 350,000 Germans absorbed almost 40 percent of the gross national product, leaving much less than was needed by the resident population of three million people. The average daily calorie intake for a Norwegian dropped from a pre-war level of 2500 calories, to 1500 calories in 1942, and to only 1237 calories by 1945. Clothing, shoes and other commodities were also hard to find and were expensive. Many goods were bartered or were available only on the black market. Leather disappeared completely and some shoes were fashioned of paper uppers and wooden soles. City parks were divided into garden plots. During and after the war Inga's sister Marie and other relatives sent packages from America to supplement the Bergs' food supplies.

Hitler stationed more troops per capita in Norway than in any other country, and buttressed Atlantic coastal defenses, because he saw *Festung Norwegen* (Fortress Norway) as a bastion against an Allied invasion of northern Europe. The Norwegian medical resources were strained by the extra numbers and by the constant conflict between the occupiers and the resistance fighters. Nurses were busy in hospitals, treating cases of malnutrition and related illnesses as well as injured soldiers. The demand for pediatric nurses like Inga was exacerbated by the more than 9,000 additional children born of Norwegian women impregnated by German soldiers.

THE CROWN PRINCESS RALLIES AMERICAN SUPPORT FOR NORWAY

Märtha and the children lived at Pook's Hill for the five-year duration of the war. Prince Olav was occasionally able to leave his post in England to join his family in America, and in 1942 Märtha was able to make a trip to London, but she was otherwise energetically promoting Norway's war needs. She was very active in American Friends of Norway, an organization started by Marie Norton Whitney Harriman, the wife of U.S. Special Envoy W. Averell Harriman. That group supported the American Red Cross, which worked through the Swedish Red Cross to funnel goods into occupied Norway.

Märtha was at the Norwegian Embassy nearly every week and she toured throughout the United States and Canada speaking about the needs of Norway's war effort. A highlight of her campaign came on September 16, 1942 at Washington's Anacostia Waterfront Naval Yard, when President Roosevelt presented to her a submarine chaser for Norway's navy. The ship was christened HMS *King Haakon VII of Norway*. The President then gave his famous "Look to Norway" speech in which he recommended Norway as a model to the rest of the free world for its courage and persistence in resisting Nazi domination: "If there is anyone who still wonders why this war is being fought, let him look to Norway. If there is anyone who has any delusions that this war could have been averted, let him look to Norway; and if there is anyone who doubts the democratic will to win, again I say, let him look to Norway…"

NORWAY, AN IMPORTANT ALLY

Norway remained heavily occupied by Germans for the entire war, but Norwegians nonetheless made significant contributions to the allied effort. By the end of April, 1940, all private Norwegian shipping companies were consolidated into *Nortraship*, the world's largest shipping fleet, with over 1,000 vessels and 30,000 crew, which was transporting munitions and supplies from North America to European allies; a total of 3,670 sailors and 706 ships from this fleet were ultimately lost to enemy action. Over British objections, Norwegians firmly maintained directorship of the fleet from primary offices in London and New York.

The Norwegian government, working from London, built up its army, navy and air force. The army was trained in Scotland and reserved for action in Norway. Norwegian and British commando units performed raids within Norway. The air force trained initially in Canada, and then Norwegian squadrons flew missions from North Weald located just outside of London. The Royal Norwegian Navy consisted of 52 vessels at war's end. It participated in wartime duties such as convoy escort and submarine detection, often distinguishing itself in battle.

Victory in Europe

On April 12, 1945 President Roosevelt died and Norway lost a good friend and bene- factor. Less than a month later on May 7, Germany surrendered. May 8 was celebrated as Victory in Europe Day. That same day, *Reichskommissar* Josef Terboven committed suicide at the Skaugum estate by detonating 50 kilograms of dynamite. On May 11 Terje Rollem of the Norwegian Army and underground resistance

A large crowd at the harbor in Oslo welcomed the Royal Family back to Norway on June 7, 1945, exactly five years after they escaped to England in 1940. From the left, King Haakon, Crown Princess Märtha, Princesses Ragnhild and Astrid, Prince Harald and Crown Prince Olav.

formally received the German surrender at the Akershus Fortress. Later on, Vidkun Quisling and 24 other traitors were imprisoned at the fortress and were eventually tried, convicted and then Quisling and two of his ministers were executed by firing squad.

Students climbed aboard a truck in Oslo to celebrate the end of World War II.

In June of the previous year King Haakon had transferred his duties as Commander of Norwegian armed forces to his son Olav. On May 13 Crown Prince Olav, in military regalia, along with five government ministers returned to Oslo and, after a triumphant motorcade, supervised the beginning of the Norwegian recovery. On June 7, 1945, five years to the day after the government had departed for England, the King and the Norwegian Royal Family returned to Oslo on HMS *Norfolk* and were welcomed by adoring crowds.[35]

400,000 thousand people welcomed the Royal Family with ships and boats in the Oslo harbor.

PRINCE HARALD'S EDUCATION

The damage to Skaugum wrought by *Reichskommissar* Terboven was repaired and Olav, Märtha and family reestablished residence. Prince Harald attended Smestad Primary School, a Norwegian State public school. Apart from security in the hallways, his schooling was not different from other children's. The Prince participated in many sports, and as a 10-year-old, he started sailing. He had his own boat and later won regattas on *Oslofjorden*. Prince Harald continued his studies at Oslo *Katedralskole*

Prince Harald (middle) was with friends at Smestad School near Oslo in 1946.

in the sciences, and after graduation enrolled at the University of Oslo.

CROWN PRINCESS MÄRTHA

After World War II the Crown Princess was received in Norway as a true hero for her work for her country while in exile in America. Norwegians anticipated that she would be a very special queen, but it was not to be. She died of cancer in 1954, just 3 years before Olav's ascendance to the throne. She was mourned on both sides of the Atlantic. In 2005, on the occasion of the Kingdom of Norway's Centennial, a bronze statue of Crown Princess Märtha was presented by Norwegian Americans to the citizens of Norway to represent the close relationship that has existed between the two countries.

KING OLAV V

After World War II King Haakon was characteristically active and involved as the country rebuilt its infrastructure, merchant fleet and alliances. In 1949 Norway joined NATO. Complications from a fall in 1955 caused the King to be confined to a wheelchair. His health declined after that and Olav assumed more and more royal duties. King Haakon VII was 85 years old when he died in 1957.

Three generations together were photographed at the Royal Residence in Skaugum. From the left: Prince Harald, King Haakon and Crown Prince Olav.

His only child was crowned Olav V and became a very popular king. During and after the war Olav had distinguished himself as a military leader and adviser. As a king in peacetime he ruled with a common touch that endeared him to Norwegians. He participated in sports, drove his own car and often traveled alone by train to his mountain cabin, without bodyguards. Early in his reign gas and oil reserves were found under Norwegian waters, and the country was on its way to becoming the wealthiest, per capita, in the world.

CROWN PRINCE HARALD

According to the Norwegian constitution the king is commander in chief and holds the rank of general in the army and admiral in the navy. Crown Prince Harald prepared for that role by attending first the Norwegian Cavalry Officers Training School and then, like his father, the Norwegian Military Academy. He graduated in 1959 and then, as his father had thirty years earlier, he attended Balliol College at Oxford, where he studied social science, history and economics. After his studies in England, Harald returned to Oslo and assumed his position as a Deputy to the King.

On August 29, 1968 Crown Prince Harald married Sonja Haraldsen from Vinderen in Oslo, the daughter of wealthy Oslo clothing store businessman Karl Haraldsen. She became Crown Princess Sonja of Norway. Because Sonja had been born a commoner, the couple had waited nine years for permission to wed. King Olav approved the union after consulting with the Presidium of the *Storting*. Harald and Sonja had two children, Princess Märtha Louise born September 22, 1971 and Prince Haakon Magnus born July 20, 1973.

KING HARALD V: 1991 TO PRESENT

Olav, like his father, did not remarry after the death of his wife. Norway was without a queen for 53 years, from the time of Olav's mother's passing in 1938 until the end of his reign in 1991. King Olav V died on January 17, 1991 at the age of 87. There was a great spontaneous public demonstration of mourning in Norway that lasted for several days before the state funeral. Norwegians lit thousands of candles and placed them in the Royal Palace courtyard along with cards and letters.

Harald became King after his father's death. On June 23, 1991 in Nideros Cathedral at Trondheim the Royal Couple was formally installed as King Harald V and Queen Sonja. The last coronation in Norway was that of King Haakon and Queen Maud in Trondheim in 1906. King Olav and King Harald have never been crowned. They were consecrated, which in Norwegian is called *signet*. The *Storting* abolished the coronation language from the constitution in 1908. Harald continued his father's tradition of maintaining an egalitarian royal family lifestyle, and as a result has enjoyed a similar popular acceptance from the Norwegian people.

King Harald's son, Haakon Magnus, became heir to the throne at birth despite being younger than his sister Märtha Louise. The Norwegian constitution was altered in 1990 granting equal primogeniture to the Norwegian throne, to be applied to heirs to follow Haakon. "Absolute", "equal" and "lineal" primogeniture are all terms for the system that stipulated inheritance of the crown by the oldest surviving child without regard to gender. The Crown Prince and his wife Crown Princess Mette-Marit have two royal children. Princess Ingrid Alexandra, who was born in January 2004, became Norway's first-ever female heir to the throne. Her younger brother, Prince Sverre Magnus was born in December 2005 but, unlike her female predecessors, Princess Ingrid remained in direct line to the throne.

Norway has shaped the monarchy to reflect the evolution of its society. In the early twentieth century Inga Berg saw her sisters Marie and Thea leave agrarian Norway, in part because they knew that their younger brother Ola would inherit their father's property. Twenty-five years later at the Skaugum Royal Residence, Nurse

This wedding photograph was taken in 2001 when Crown Prince Haakon Magnus (King Harald and Queen Sonja's son) married Mette-Marit Tjessem Høiby, a commoner. They are from the left: Sven O. Høiby and Marit Tjessem (parents of Mette-Marit), Crown Prince Haakon, Queen Sonja, King Harald and Princess Märtha-Louise (daughter of King Harald and Queen Sonja).

Inga Berg looked on as Princesses Ragnhild and Astrid played with their *Lillebror,* resigned to their lots in the shadow of that future king. At the beginning of the twenty-first century a female heir to the throne is the symbol of a society where 80 percent of women are employed and women have recently held top government positions including Supreme Court Justice, Minister of Defense, and Prime Minister. Determined and successful women like Inga Berg are no longer exceptions in Norway.[36]

INGA BERG: 1945 TO THE END OF HER LIFE

After the war Inga Berg continued her private practice in Oslo. She mostly counseled with mothers in well-to-do families, delivered their babies and, as she had at Skaugum, served as a pediatric nurse-in-residence. During her last working years she filled less stressful positions as a consulting nurse in hospitals that were connected to retirement centers.

Inga Berg was dressed in a Valdres *bunad,* a folk dress made in the Valdres style.

Inga never married, but she liked to say that her family consisted of the many children she cared for during her 40 years of nursing. Her life was not without romance, for she maintained a close thirty-year relationship with Lars Printz, a well-known Oslo painter of portraits and landscapes in oil. Several of his works adorned her home. In retirement Inga returned to her house in Bagn, where she lived alone, although in proximity to family members.

Public interest at special times in the life of Prince Harald brought attention to Inga, and over the years she was interviewed for several newspaper articles. She attended the Prince's confirmation and wedding, and for the latter she hand-embroidered a bell sash as a gift to the royal couple.[37] When Harald and Sonja's son Haakon Magnus was born, Inga sent him a special present with a story that probably delighted his father. The gift was a pair of socks that she had originally hand-knit at Skaugum for baby Harald, and then saved after he outgrew them.

Lars Printz, a renowned landscape and portrait painter in oil shared with Inga Berg an enduring thirty-year friendship.

King Haakon posed for a portrait painted by Lars Printz in 1937 during the time he met Inga for the first time.

Inga lived in her Midtberg house in Bagn as long as she was able and then went to the nearby Sør-Aurdal retirement home in Bagn. There she was in residence for about five more years and enjoyed requests to tell about her time at Skaugum. Inga Berg passed away on November 9, 1983 at the age of 87. She did not live to attend the 1991 consecration of Harald V, but was remembered as a very early influence in the development of the King.

PART IV

Endnotes, Appendices, Bibliography & Credits

*Inga held up a pair of wool socks she knit
for Prince Harald as a baby. She kept them and then
sent them back to him for his first son, Haakon Magnus.*

ENDNOTES

▶ **PART I**

1. *"Jeg var Prins Harald's barnepike"* (I was Prince Harald's Nanny) *Hjemmet* (the Home), October 23, 1968, 34-49. This 16-page feature article, which included photos taken by Inga Berg, appeared in this well-known Norwegian national magazine. Her reason for consenting to be interviewed for this article in 1968, 30 years after she left Skaugum, was to fund a trip to the United States to visit her four siblings: Marie (Berg) Bjerkness, Thea (Berg) Gunderson, Arne and Gunnar Berg. This account led the author to inquire about the location of the original copy of Inga's journal. Ragnhild Berg, the wife of the author's now deceased cousin, Martin Berg, was given all of Inga's papers after Inga died in 1983; Ragnhild retains possession of the original copy at her home in Fåberg, near Lillehammer, Norway.

The term "nanny" used in the title of the article above means something very different to American readers than to Norwegians. For Americans, the term is used very loosely, meaning everything from baby sitter, mother's helper, *au pair* to governess and uncertified or certified children's nurse. However, Norwegians who translate it, use *barnepike* as they find it in the dictionary translated as nursemaid or nanny. The word they should have used is *barnepleierske* a trained (certified) children's nurse. A further distinction is made: an infant nurse cares for children until they can walk and at that point a children's nurse takes over. Even in Norwegian, this word is sometimes confused, at least by some, to mean the same as *jordmor* (midwife) who is basically a certified or uncertified midwife helping the mother in the delivery of the baby. Often the midwife works in conjunction with a medical doctor either at home or at a hospital. Sometimes the *jordmor* may stay on in the household for a few days after the birth. Inga was trained both as a midwife and as an infant nurse and it is in this sense of the word that nanny is used in this book.

Brain development is an emerging topic of great interest in education circles, in both Norway and the United States. It is evident that early learning from birth to age three is becoming a focal point in educational research. Studies have indicated that by the age of three, eighty percent of the child's brain cells have been formed. This information supports the importance of Inga Berg's impact on Prince Harald. See: Charles A. Nelson, Professor of Pediatrics at Harvard Medical School and his book with M. de Haan and K.M. Thomas: *Neuroscience and Cognitive Development: The Role of Experience and the Developing Brain* (New York: John Wiley and Sons, 2006).

2. *"Prins Haralds dåb"* (Prince Harald's Baptism), *Aftenposten*, March 31, 1937, 1.

3. For an excellent history of this era, see: Else Roesdahl, *The Vikings* (London: Penguin Press Books, 1998), 9-22.

4. A concise history of Norway is found in John Midgaard's book, *A Brief History of Norway* (Oslo: Tano, 1986), 76-118. Note: the following pages of Part I are referenced to this work as well as to Stenersen, below, up to the section on Inga Berg.

5. Øivind Stenersen and Ivar Libæk, *The History of Norway: From the Ice Age to Today* (Lysaker: Dinamo Forlag, 2003), 67-121.

6. Tor Bomann-Larsen, *Folket: Haakon & Maud, II* (The Nation: Haakon and Maud, II) (Oslo, J.W. Cappelens Forlag, 2004), l26-346.

7. David H. Lovett, the Warden and historian, of St. Edmund's related a common occurrence on Sundays: The royal carriage would drive from the Palace down Karl Johans Gate dropping off

King Haakon at the *Domkirke* and then driving a few blocks north to St. Edmund's where Queen Maud would attend the 11:00 service. Queen Maud was a very generous member, contributing yearly to the church budget and establishing the "Queen Maud Fund for the Poor in Oslo". In 1906, the month of her coronation, she gave gifts of a gold cross and a pair of candlesticks for the main altar. In 1938 she gave a "Plaque of Christ" which was the personal possession of her mother, Queen Alexandra of England. After Queen Maud died in 1938, King Haakon dedicated a white marble tablet in front of the church lectern reading, "In Loving remembrance of my beloved wife, Maud, Queen of Norway" T.K. Derry, *A History of St Edmund's Church: 1884-1974* (Oslo: Merkantile Trykkeri, 1976), 66-79.

8. Kjell Arnljot Wig, *Kongen ser Tilbake* (The King Looks Back) (Oslo: J.W. Cappelens Forlag, 1977), 11-90.

9. Arvid Møller, *Kronprinsess Märtha, Hustru-mor-medmenneske* (Crown Princess Märtha, Wife, Mother, Human Being) (Oslo: J.W. Cappelens Forlag, 1990), 11-90.

10. Jon Ola Gjermundsen, *Gard og bygd i Sør-Aurdal, Bind A, Reinli og Vestre Bagn* (Farm and Community in South Aurdal, Vol. A, Reinli and West Bagn) (Sør-Aurdal Kommune Valdres: Bygdeboks Forlag, 1977), 667-698.

11. Information came from informal interviews both in Norway and Minnesota over several years (2002-present) but the primary interviewees were John Berg of Hønefoss and Anne Marie and Per Gabrielsen of Bagn. For a detailed list, see preface, bibliography, emails and notes in possession of the author.

12. *"Afgangsvidnesbyrd"* (School Graduation Report) was issued to Marie Berg by Nils D. Lie, Bagn school official, April 28, 1906. Also extant is a companion document for Thea Berg for 1907. A similar document was issued to Inga Berg but has not been found at time of publication. Both documents are in possession of the author.

13. On the postcard from Marie Berg to Inga Berg on April 29, 1912, she wrote on the front side of the card: "Here you see we have come only as far as Southampton." Marie and her sister, Thea, were rerouted to Liverpool and boarded the SS *Cedric* for New York. The picture postcard of the ship, *Olympic*, the ship they were supposed to take to New York, is now in possession of the author and the translation is by the author.

14. *Jordmorutdanningen: Gjordemor, Jordemor, Jordmor: 175år Jordmorskolen i Oslo* (Midwife Training: Midwife, Midwife, Midwife: 175 Years at the Midwife School in Oslo) [The three different spellings indicate the change in the Norwegian language during this period of time.] (Oslo: Jordmorutdanningen, 1993), 96-110.

15. *"Inga fra Sør-Aurdal var barnepleierske for Arveprins Harald"* (Inga from South Aurdal was a Children's Nurse for Crown Prince Harald), *Oppland Arbeiderblad*, February 4, 1983, no. 5, np.

16. Dr. Kr. Brandt, *Lærebok for Jordmore* (Textbook for Midwives) (Kristiania: Forlag av H. Aschehoug, 1913), 1-431.

17. Florence Nightingale, *Notes on Nursing: What It is and What It Is Not* (Philadelphia: Lippincott, 1992), Introduction, unpaginated.

18. Kari Melby, *Kall og Kamp: Norsk Sykepleierforbunds Historie* (Vocation and Struggle: History of the Norwegian Nurses Association) (Oslo: J.W. Cappelens Forlag, 1990), 17-117.

19. Email interviews with Annabelle Despard, the sister of Anita Despard for whom Inga was the midwife and then children's nurse beginning October 4, 1927. Emails dated 2006-2007 are in possession of the author.

20. Inga Berg, *Dagbok av Inga Berg 1937-1938* (Journal of Inga Berg 1937-1938), unpaginated.

21. Yngve Woxworth, ed., *Kongeboliger og Nasjonalskatter i Norge* (The King's Residences and Other National Treasures) (Oslo: Hjemmenes Forlag, 1978), 26-33.

22. *"Skaugum: Her Skal De Bo"* ("Skaugum: Here They Shall Live"), *Hjemmet*, September, 1968, 2-28.

23. Geir Thomas Risåsen, *The Royal Palace* (Oslo: Andresen & Butenschøn, 2005), 6-17.

▶ **PART III**

24. Wig, 171-174.

25. *"Jeg var Konprins Haralds barnepike," Hjemmet*, 1958, 34-42.

26. Johs Andenæs, Olav Riste, and Magne Skodvin, *Norway and the Second World War* (Oslo: Aschehoug, 1996), 54-91.

27. "Nazis in Norway," *New York Times*, April 9, 1940, 1. Reportage is based on wire services of The United Press, *The New York Times* and Reuters. See also: William Shirer, *Challenge of Scandinavia* (Toronto: Little Brown and Co., 1946), 37.

28. "London Hears of Invasion," *New York Times*, April 9, 1940, 2. See also: Florence Jaffray Hurst Harrimann, *Mission to the North* (Philadelphia: J.B. Lippincott Co., 1941).

29. Shirer, 38.

30. Amanda Johnson, *Norway, Her Invasion and Occupation* (Decatur, GA: Bowen Press, 1948), 159-163.

31. Andreas Hauge and Knut Werner Hagen, *Bagn 1940* (Oslo: Forvars Museet, 2001), 86-166. The section on the Bagn episode is referenced to this work.

32. Personal interview with Arnfinn and Mary Ann Rosenlund, Edina, Minnesota, April 20, 2007. Mr. Rosenlund was 22 years old in 1940 and became active in the Norwegian Resistance during World War II. He was a taxi and ambulance driver in Bagn, which afforded him the opportunity to be out and about, all the while furnishing information to the Resistance as obtained from his various vantage points. Mr. Rosenlund emigrated to Minnesota after World War II, married an American, Mary Ann, and became a building contractor, among whose employees was Arne Berg, brother of Inga Berg. He is now 89 years old.

33. "Haakon Defends [the] Course," *New York Times* (August 27, 1940), 4.

34. Joanne Romansie, "Look to Norway," *News from Norway* (Washington D.C.: Norwegian Embassy and Consulates General, winter, 2005), 6-7. For a more detailed treatment of this era and Princess Märtha's life, see also, Steinar Hybertsen, *Crown Princess Märtha: The American Story* [DVD] (Seattle: Norwegian American Foundation, 2006).

35. Møller, 197-272. See also, "Fanfare Omitted by Royal Request," *New York Times* August 29, 1940, 3.

36. Stenerson and Libæk, 121-180.

37. *"Haralds barnepike ga klokkestreng"* (Harald's Children's Nurse Gave a Bellpull Hanging) [for the royal wedding] *Hjemmet*, September 18, 1968, np. Bellpulls or bell ropes were used to ring bells but have evolved to become decorative wall hangings made with traditional Norwegian designs. Inga spent over 100 hours needle pointing this gift.

APPENDIX 1

LINEAGE OF NORWEGIAN MONARCHS

Usage of Royal Titles

There is no consistency among writers in their use of European royal titles. In fact genealogists list eight different forms. In Norway, the titles used most commonly are King/Queen plus first name or formally His/Her Royal Highness (HRH). Another variant in formal writing is to use His/Her Majesty (HM). The title, Crown Prince/Princess, is used only if that person is next in line to become sovereign; otherwise just Prince/Princess is the practice. The five titles used in Norway are: King/Queen, His/Her Majesty (HM), His/Her Royal Highness (HRH), Crown Prince/Princess (CP) and Prince/Princess.

FIRST GENERATION

HRH King Haakon VII of Norway was born in 1872 as HRH Prince Christian Frederik Carl George Valdemar Axel of Denmark. He was the son of King Christian Frederick VIII of Denmark and Princess Louise Josephine Eugénie of Sweden. The Norwegian parliament asked him to become King of Norway and upon doing so, he changed his name to Haakon. King Haakon died in 1957 at age 85, in Oslo, having lived 19 years longer than Queen Maud.

HRH Queen Maud was born in 1869 as HRH Princess Maud Charlotte Mary Victoria of the United Kingdom of Great Britain and Ireland. She was a daughter of Edward VII of the United Kingdom and Princess Alexandra Caroline Marie Charlotte Louise Julia of Denmark. In 1896 she married Prince Carl and when he was chosen to become King of Norway in 1905, she became the new Queen. She died in London in 1938 at the age of 68

SECOND GENERATION

HRH King Olav V of Norway was born in 1903 as HRH Prince Alexander Edward Christian Frederick of Denmark. His parents were to become King Haakon VII and Queen Maud. After November 1905, at age two, he became HRH Crown Prince Olav of Norway. He became King of Norway in 1957. He won a gold medal in sailing for Norway in the 1928 Summer Olympic Games. He also ski jumped competitively at *Holmenkollen,* a famous ski jumping hill in Oslo. He died in 1991 at the age of 87, having lived 37 years longer than Crown Princess Märtha.

HRH Princess Märtha was born in 1901 as HRH Princess Märtha Sofia Lovisa Dagmar Thyra of Sweden. Her parents were Prince Carl Vilhelm of Sweden and Princess Ingeborg Charlotte Caroline Frederikka of Denmark. She was a cousin of Count Folke Bernadotte of Sweden and a cousin of Crown Prince Olav. Crown Princess Märtha married Prince Olav in 1929. She died in 1954 at age 53 after a long illness.

THIRD GENERATION

HRH King Harald V of Norway was born in 1937 as HRH Prince Harald of Norway. He was the son of Crown Prince Olav V and Crown Princess Märtha. Prince Harald represented Norway in the 5.5-meter yacht sailing class during the Summer Olympics in 1964, 1968 and 1972. He became King of Norway in 1991; his ascendancy to kingship was the first time in nearly 600 years that a monarch born on Norwegian soil became king.

HRH Queen Sonja was born in 1937 in Oslo as Sonja Haraldsen, a commoner, and daughter of a wealthy Oslo merchant. According to Rule 36 of the Norwegian Constitution, a Prince of the Royal House may not marry a commoner without consent of the king. King Olav V consulted with members of the Government and the Storting and after 10 years of waiting, granted Harald and Sonja permission to marry and thereby avoided constitutional questions.

Princess Ragnhild Alexandra of Norway was born in 1930, the daughter of Crown Prince Olav and Crown Princess Märtha. She was the first Norwegian Princess to marry in more than 600 years; her husband is Erling Sven Lorentzen, a commoner.

Princess Astrid Maud Ingeborg of Norway was born in 1932, the daughter of Crown Prince Olav and Crown Princess Märtha. She married Johan Martin Ferner, a commoner, in 1961. Since Harald's two sisters Ragnhild and Astrid, were married in civil ceremonies, they have not been given the title "Royal Highness," by King Harald but each has retained the title of Princess.

FOURTH GENERATION

HRH Haakon Magnus is the son of King Harald and Queen Sonja and was born in Oslo in 1973. He is a third cousin of King Carl Gustaf of Sweden.

Crown Princess Mette Marit is the wife of Crown Prince Haakon Magnus and was born a commoner in Kristiansand, Norway in 1973. King Harald has given her the title "Crown Princess".

Princess Märtha Louise is the daughter of King Harald and Queen Sonja and was born in 1971. She relinquished the title of Royal Highness with approval of HM King Harald in 2002, when she began a cultural relations enterprise. Later that year she married writer Ari Mikael Behn.

FIFTH GENERATION

HRH Princess Ingrid Alexandra is the daughter of Crown Prince Haakon Magnus and Crown Princess Mette-Marit and was born in Norway in 2004. She is next in line to Crown Prince Haakon Magnus to become Queen of Norway. The Norwegian Constitution was amended in 1990 to allow the throne of Norway to be inherited by the first-born child of either gender.

HRH Prince Sverre Magnus is the son of Crown Prince Haakon Magnus and Crown Princess Mette-Marit and was born in 2005.

Maud Angelica is the daughter of Märtha Louise and Ari Behn and was born in 2003.

Leah Isadora is the second daughter of Märtha Louise and Ari Behn and was born in 2005.

Emma Tallulah is the third daughter of of Märtha Louise and Ari Behn and was born in 2008.

Marius is the son of Crown Princess Mette-Marit from a previous relationship and was born in 1996. He has no titles nor is he in line of succession to the Norwegian throne.

APPENDIX 2

PEDIGREE OF KING HARALD V

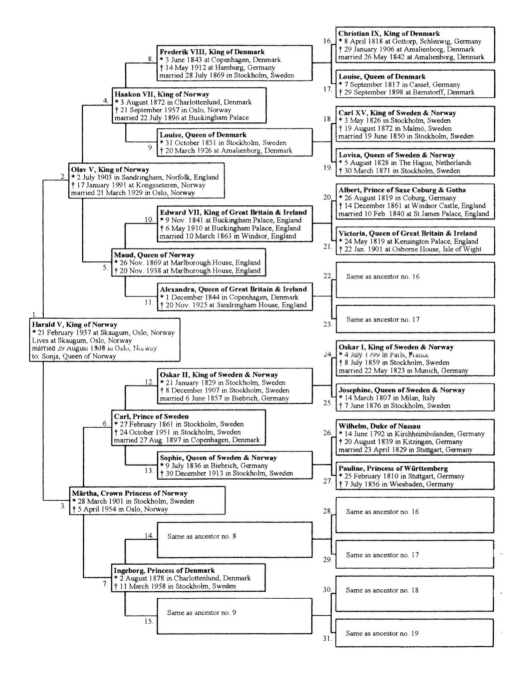

Christian IX, King of Denmark
16.
* 8 April 1818 at Gottorp, Schleswig, Germany
† 29 January 1906 at Amalienborg, Denmark
married 26 May 1842 at Amalienborg, Denmark

Frederik VIII, King of Denmark
8.
* 3 June 1843 at Copenhagen, Denmark
† 14 May 1912 at Hamburg, Germany
married 28 July 1869 in Stockholm, Sweden

Louise, Queen of Denmark
17.
* 7 September 1817 in Cassel, Germany
† 29 September 1898 at Bernstorff, Denmark

Haakon VII, King of Norway
4.
* 3 August 1872 in Charlottenlund, Denmark
† 21 September 1957 in Oslo, Norway
married 22 July 1896 at Buckingham Palace

Carl XV, King of Sweden & Norway
18.
* 3 May 1826 in Stockholm, Sweden
† 19 August 1872 in Malmö, Sweden
married 19 June 1850 in Stockholm, Sweden

Louise, Queen of Denmark
9.
* 31 October 1851 in Stockholm, Sweden
† 20 March 1926 at Amalienborg, Denmark

Lovisa, Queen of Sweden & Norway
19.
* 5 August 1828 in The Hague, Netherlands
† 30 March 1871 in Stockholm, Sweden

Olav V, King of Norway
2.
* 2 July 1903 in Sandringham, Norfolk, England
† 17 January 1991 at Kongsseteren, Norway
married 21 March 1929 in Oslo, Norway

Albert, Prince of Saxe Coburg & Gotha
20.
* 26 August 1819 in Coburg, Germany
† 14 December 1861 at Windsor Castle, England
married 10 Feb. 1840 at St James Palace, England

Edward VII, King of Great Britain & Ireland
10.
* 9 Nov. 1841 at Buckingham Palace, England
† 6 May 1910 at Buckingham Palace, England
married 10 March 1863 in Windsor, England

Victoria, Queen of Great Britain & Ireland
21.
* 24 May 1819 at Kensington Palace, England
† 22 Jan. 1901 at Osborne House, Isle of Wight

Maud, Queen of Norway
5.
* 26 Nov. 1869 at Marlborough House, England
† 20 Nov. 1938 at Marlborough House, England

Alexandra, Queen of Great Britain & Ireland
11.
* 1 December 1844 in Copenhagen, Denmark
† 20 Nov. 1925 at Sandringham House, England

22.
Same as ancestor no. 16

23.
Same as ancestor no. 17

1.
Harald V, King of Norway
* 21 February 1937 at Skaugum, Oslo, Norway
Lives at Skaugum, Oslo, Norway
married 29 August 1968 in Oslo, Norway
to: Sonja, Queen of Norway

Oskar I, King of Sweden & Norway
24.
* 4 July 1799 in Paris, France
† 8 July 1859 in Stockholm, Sweden
married 22 May 1823 in Munich, Germany

Oskar II, King of Sweden & Norway
12.
* 21 January 1829 in Stockholm, Sweden
† 8 December 1907 in Stockholm, Sweden
married 6 June 1857 in Biebrich, Germany

Josephine, Queen of Sweden & Norway
25.
* 14 March 1807 in Milan, Italy
† 7 June 1876 in Stockholm, Sweden

Carl, Prince of Sweden
6.
* 27 February 1861 in Stockholm, Sweden
† 24 October 1951 in Stockholm, Sweden
married 27 Aug. 1897 in Copenhagen, Denmark

Wilhelm, Duke of Nassau
26.
* 14 June 1792 in Kirchheimbolanden, Germany
† 20 August 1839 in Kitzingen, Germany
married 23 April 1829 in Stuttgart, Germany

Sophie, Queen of Sweden & Norway
13.
* 9 July 1836 in Biebrich, Germany
† 30 December 1913 in Stockholm, Sweden

Pauline, Princess of Württemberg
27.
* 25 February 1810 in Stuttgart, Germany
† 7 July 1856 in Wiesbaden, Germany

Märtha, Crown Princess of Norway
3.
* 28 March 1901 in Stockholm, Sweden
† 5 April 1954 in Oslo, Norway

28.
Same as ancestor no. 16

14.
Same as ancestor no. 8

29.
Same as ancestor no. 17

Ingeborg, Princess of Denmark
7.
* 2 August 1878 in Charlottenlund, Denmark
† 11 March 1958 in Stockholm, Sweden

30.
Same as ancestor no. 18

15.
Same as ancestor no. 9

31.
Same as ancestor no. 19

APPENDIX 3

SIGNIFICANT EVENTS IN THE LIFE OF PRINCE HARALD AND INGA BERG

1869	Princess Maud (1869-1938) is born in Marlborough House, England. She became the first Norwegian Queen in the modern era.
1872	Prince Carl of Denmark (1872-1957) is born. He will become King Haakon VII of Norway.
1896	Prince Carl of Denmark and Princess Maud of England are married at Buckingham Palace, London, England.
1896	Inga Berg (1896-1983) is born in Bagn, Valdres, Norway.
1901	Crown Princess Märtha (1901-1954) is born in Stockholm, Sweden.
1903	Prince Olav V (1903-1991) is born in Sandringham, Norfolk, England, to Princess Maud and Prince Carl.
1905-1957	Prince Carl of Denmark becomes King Haakon VII, the first independent Norwegian king in nearly 600 years.
1929	Crown Prince Olav marries Princess Märtha of Sweden in Oslo, Norway.
1930	Ragnhild is born. She is the first princess born on Norwegian soil in almost 600 years.
1932	Astrid, the second daughter, is born.
1937	Inga becomes pediatric nurse for Prince Harald when he is 17 days old. She was the first Norwegian children's nurse in the Royal Family. He was the first future king born on Norwegian soil in almost 600 years.
1938	Inga leaves her position with the Royal Family. Her journal details her time as nurse for Prince Harald.
1938	Queen Maud dies in London at Marlborough House in England at age of 69.
1940	Germans invade Norway. King Haakon and Crown Prince Olav are evacuated to England; Crown Princess Märtha and children escape to the U.S.
1940-1945	German occupation of Norway: Norwegian, Vidkun Quisling, worked with the Germans; cruel treatment of Norwegians in Norway.
June 7, 1945	The Royal Family returns to Norway.
1953	Crown Princess Märtha dies at age of 53. She is buried in Akershus Castle in Oslo.
1957	King Haakon dies. Crown Prince Olav becomes the second Norwegian king (1957-1991) in the modern era.
1958	The first major article about Inga Berg appears in *Hjemmet*. It was the first in a series of publications about Inga's life with the Royal Family.
1968	Crown Prince Harald marries a commoner, Sonja Haraldsen, from Oslo.

1971	Princess Märtha Louise is born to Crown Prince Harald and Crown Princess Sonja. Märtha Louise later relinquished the use of the title of Royal Highness when she launched her career in cultural relations.
1973	Prince Haakon Magnus, future king, is born to Crown Prince Harald and Crown Princess Sonja.
1973	Mette-Marit Tjessem Høiby, a commoner, is born at Kristiansand, Norway. She will become the wife of Prince Haakon.
1983	Inga Berg dies at the age of 87 in Bagn, Valdres where she was born.
1990	The Norwegian Constitution is amended to grant equal primogeniture to the Norwegian throne. The amendment stipulates inheritance of the crown by the oldest surviving child without regard to gender.
1991	King Olav dies and Harald becomes king. Harald is the present King of Norway and the first king born on Norwegian soil in almost 600 years.
2001	Crown Prince Haakon Magnus, the future king of Norway, marries Mette-Marit Tjessem Høiby in Oslo.
2004	Princess Ingrid Alexandra, the first Norwegian queen to be born on Norwegian soil in 600 years, is born.
2005	Prince Sverre Magnus is born to Crown Prince Haakon Magnus and Crown Princess Mette-Marit.

APPENDIX 4

INGA'S DOCUMENTS

Newspaper article, *Tidens Tegn*, 1937

SHE WHO WILL CARE FOR THE PRINCE.

"I will take care of him the same way as I would take care of any other child!" says Prince Harald's new nurse Inga Berg."

The midwife who assisted in the delivery of the Prince, the first heir to the throne born in Norway in almost 600 years, is Anne Koren who has already received praise for her work.

The woman who will now be appearing in the news is Inga Berg. She was pediatric nurse for 15 years before she got the great honor of caring for His Royal Highness the heir Prince Harald of Norway.

Infant nurse Inga Berg is from Bagn in Valdres and received her training as a midwife at the Women's Clinic. She later worked as an infant nurse including three years in collaboration with the renowned [Dr.] E.I. Lloyd. Since then Miss Berg worked as a private nurse here in Oslo under the leadership of midwife Mrs. Thomassen. Midwife Thomassen is reputed to have said to her pupil when the great honor was announced to her: "You should care for the Prince just as you would care for any child, Nurse Inga!"

How did you get this job?

"I have worked for several friends of the Crown Princess," says Nurse Inga, "and most recently, or I mean currently, at Mrs. Tjerslands, who recommended me. It was settled a month ago, and I'll be starting around the 10th – 15th of March and will be in their service for an indefinite time."

Have you ever taken care of royal children before?

"Not exactly, but I once cared for a child whom Queen Maud carried in the baptismal ceremony. The mother was a Mrs. Despard, neé Hurum."

One should not believe this honor has gone to Nurse Inga's head. Far from it. The Crown Princess knows what she's doing. Infant nurse Inga Berg makes an unusually good impression.

"I was not at all prepared for all of this," she says quietly. "It is a great honor and I'm much looking forward to working at Skaugum. It will be both exciting and fun."

What will the Crown Prince's life be like during the first weeks?

"It will be only sleep and eat, eat and sleep for the first three weeks. He will be changed and bathed around 7:00 in the morning and will be fed every three hours. After about three weeks, he will be able to go outside, and it will be exciting when others can see him."

Have you seen him?

"No, but I've heard he resembles Princess Ragnhild."

How do you feel about being the one who will care for Norway's first future crown prince?

That was a question nurse Inga was not ready to answer at this time.

Oppland Arbeiderblad article: February 4, 1983

VALDRES LADY TOOK CARE OF THE CROWN PRINCE WHEN HE WAS LITTLE....

We met Inga Berg, a genuine woman from Bagn, at Solås convalescent hospital.

It is evident that a special story can be told about this charming older woman. She can tell about living at Skaugum when she was young, when she took care of Crown Prince Olav's child. We're immediately interested in finding out whether today's Prince and Princesses were well-behaved as children.

"Oh yes, that I can say for sure. Crown Prince Harald, was little more than a week old when I first came to Skaugum. I'll never forget how beautiful Crown Princess Märtha was when she welcomed me. Her happiest moment was giving birth to Harald. I was in charge of all of Harald's care; I even slept by him at night. The days I had off, the Crown Princess would take care of him herself."

Did you also care for the two princesses?

"Basically, caring for Harald was my only duty, but I would watch them as well if the other staff were off. And they were so well behaved, all three of them."

How long did you stay at Skaugum?

"Almost two years, I left right before the Second World War."

You must have a lot of valuable memories from this time Miss Berg; not many people can say that they have shared a house with the Royal Family.

"What I remember best is Christmas Eve in 1937. I had Queen Maud and Crown Princess Märtha by my side during the dinner, with the rest of the royal family around us. This was a big moment for me. The Queen was very sweet. I once took a picture of Harald, and Crown Princess Märtha had to send it to Queen Maud, who was in England at the time..."

"I have a wall at home which I call 'the royal wall', and there they are, one after another, the whole royal family," recounts Inga Berg.

As is meet and proper, we would like to know Miss Berg's feelings about the Crown Prince's engagement.

"Oh, I sent them a telegram, and I think it was nice to see the Crown Prince so happy. Harald was very attached to his mother, and her death was a heavy loss for him. He mourned her passing for a long time. She was an exceptional human being. The last time I saw Crown Princess Märtha was at Crown Prince Harald's confirmation."

You mentioned the confirmation; are you also going to the wedding this fall?

"I'm waiting a little. I just hope my health will be good enough for me to be able to attend. I've already started making the wedding present, but what it is will remain a secret for now," says Inga Berg with a smile.

A T T E S T.

Fröken Inga BERG har vært ansatt som spedbarnpleierske på Skaugum fra 10/3-1937 - 31/7-1938.

Hun har i dette tidsrum forestått alt arbeide i forbindelse med stell og pleie av Prins Harald og har utført disse sine plikter på en utmerket måte.

Fröken Berg har vist sig som en særdeles dyktig spedbarnpleierske; hun er meget pålitelig og ordentlig og vel inne i sitt spesielle fag, så man trygt har kunnet overlate til henne selvstendig å utföre sitt arbeide og H.K.H. Kronprinsessen har vært meget vel tilfreds med hennes tjeneste.

Hun slutter nu i sin stilling på Skaugum idet der for Prins Harald er ansatt en vanlig barnepike, da der for hans vedkommende ikke lenger er behov for spedbarnstell.

Fröken Berg gis hermed den beste anbefaling.

N. R. Østgaard.

LETTER OF RECOMMENDATION

Miss Inga Berg has been employed as an infant nurse at Skaugum in the period 3/10/1937 to 7/31/1938.

She has in this time managed all work regarding the prince's care and tending, and has carried out her duties in an excellent way.

Miss Berg has proven herself an exceptionally competent infant nurse. She is very reliable and orderly. She knows her special field very well, so well that she has been left to independently perform her duties, and Her Royal Highness the Crown Princess has been very satisfied with her service.

She will now end her position here at Skaugum, as a regular nanny has been engaged to take care of Prince Harald now that he no longer needs special infant care.

Miss Berg is hereby given the best recommendations.

Signature   N.R. Østgaard

H. K. H. KRONPRINSENS SEKRETÆR

E.

OSLO SLOTT, 11. August 1938.

Fröken Inga Berg.
c/o Herr Skredder Berg.
Bagn.

Jeg tillater mig herved å oversende i kontanter kr.110,- utgjörende

feriegodtgjörelse for 14 dager	kr. 75,-
kostpenger for 14 dager à kr. 2,50	" 35,-
	kr.110,-

Jeg skulde være takknemlig for Deres erkjennelse herfor og tegner

Banko kr.110,-

ærbödigst

I. Bommen

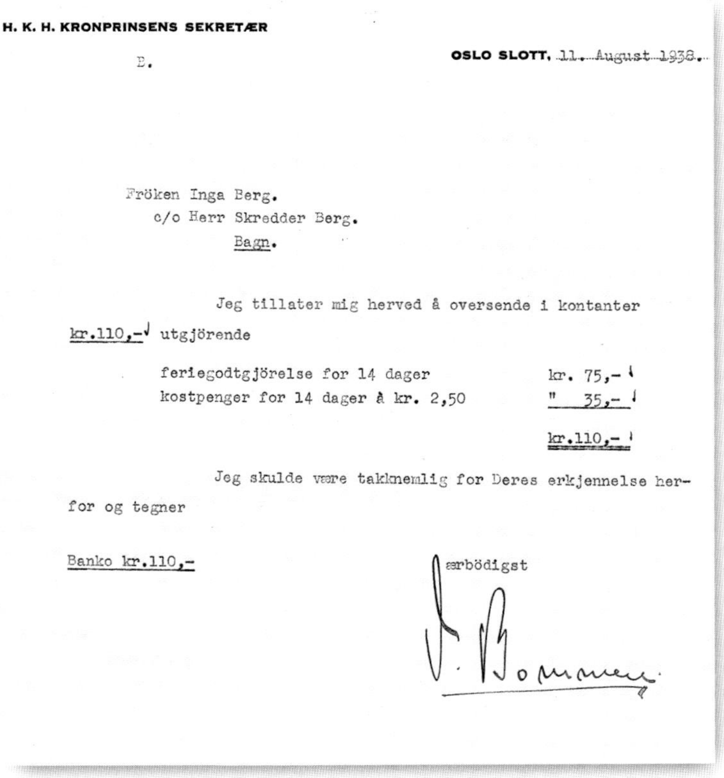

Secretary to His Royal Highness, the Crown Prince

Oslo Palace, August 11, 1938

Miss Inga Berg
c/o Mr. Berg, the Tailor

I am pleased to send herewith the sum of 110 kroner covering compensation for:

14 days of vacation time	75 kroner
Expenses for 14 days at 2.50 kroner per day	35 kroner
	110 kroner

I would be grateful for your acknowledgement of the receipt of the sum, and your signature attesting thereto.

Cash 110 kroner

Sincerely,
I. Bommen

[In today's dollars Inga would be earning roughly $730 per month plus room and board, assuming she worked continuously.]

Fru S. Inga Berg,

B a g n

I anledning av

H. K. H. Kronprins Haralds og Frøken Sonja Haraldsens

Bryllup

har H. M. Kongens Hoffmarskalk

ifølge befaling den ære å innby

S. Inga Berg

til å overvære Vielsen i Oslo Domkirke torsdag 29. august 1968 kl. 1700.

Inga Berg's personal invitation to the wedding of Crown Prince Harald and Miss Sonja Haraldson.

APPENDIX 5

EXCERPTS OF WEIGHT AND MILK CHARTS, FEBRUARY 23 – APRIL 23, 1937

Inga kept a record of Harald's weight in grams, from the time he was born (3,170 grams = about 7 pounds) until April 5 of that year. Following that, she often noted his weight in the daily accounts that she wrote in her journal.

Vekt ved fødselen	3170 gr.
23-2.	2920 „
24-2	3000 „
25-2	3030 „
26-2	3120 „
27-2	3140 „
28-2	3190 „
29-2	
1/3	3220 „
2	3260 „
3	3260 „
4	3310 „
5	3320 „
6	3390 „
7	3370 „
8	3400 „
9	3420 „
10	3460 „
11	4460 „
12	3450 „
13	3520 „
14	

15/3	Vekt	3650 gr.
17	„	3690 „
20	„	3750 „
23	„	3840 „
25	„	3860 „
27	„	3960 „
29	„	4030 „
31	„	4040 „
3/4	„	4040 „
5	„	4150 „
8	„	4140 „
10	„	4300 „
12	„	4260 „
14	„	4330 „
16	„	4330 „
19	„	4450 „
22	„	4570 „
25	„	4600 „
30	200gr ökning. „	4800 „
4/5	100 „	4900 „

Melkemengde.		Sum.
23/2.		190 gr.
24		260 „
25		400 „
26		390 „
27		460 „
28		495 „
1/3		440 „
2		490 „
3		440 „
4	Hver 4. time	470 „
5		495 „
6		530 „
7		560 „
8	15gr. kunstig.	485 „
9	20 „	540 „
10	0	520 „
11	10 „	540 „
12	0	545 „
13	65 „	535 „
14	30 „	535 „
15	15 „	535 „

16/3	140gr kunstig		570 gr.
17	75 „	— „ —	580 „
18	80 „	— „ —	570 „
19	25 „	— „ —	530 „
20	45 „	— „ —	545 „
21	125 „	— „ —	570 „
22	70 „	— „ —	550 „
23	80 „	— „ —	550 „
24	65 „	— „ —	545 „
25	90 „	— „ —	575 „
26	60 „	— „ —	560 „
27	105 „	— „ —	590 „
28	35 „	— „ —	590 „
29	55 „	— „ —	580 „
30	35 „	— „ —	590 „
31	175 „	— „ —	590 „
1/4	120 „	— „ —	585 „
2	110 „	— „ —	590 „
3	130 „	— „ —	600 „
4	90 „	— „ —	600 „
5	80 „	— „ —	600 „
6	80 „	— „ —	600 „

APPENDIX 6

CONTINUED RELATIONSHPS

After 35 years, small children's voices are once again heard in the halls at Skaugum and the Royal Palace. The author continued to have ongoing contact with both the Royal Family and his aunt Inga.

A family photograph taken at Skaugum, January 2008, shows Crown Prince Haakon Magnus and Crown Princess Mette-Marit with their children: Prince Sverre Magnus (on lap), Princess Ingrid Alexandra, and Mette-Marit's son Marius. Photo: Knut Kollandsrud. Courtesy Det Kongelige Hoff

Odell Bjerkness is standing next to Inga Berg in front of her modest home in Bagn, Valdres in May 1973 when she was 77 years old.

King Olav of Norway is greeted by Professor Bjerkness during the King's visit to Concordia College in Moorhead, Minnesota in 1986.

The Royal Family gathered at the Royal Palace for the baptism of Emma Tallulah Behn, daughter of Princess Märtha Louise and Ari Behn, January 2009. From left to right (front): Leah Isadora Behn, Princess Märtha Louise holding Emma Tallulah, and Maud Angelica Behn sitting on Ari Behn's lap. Standing behind: King Harald, Queen Sonja, Crown Princess Mette-Marit, and Crown Prince Haakon Magnus.

Photo: Cathrine Wessel. Courtesy Det Kongelige Hoff

Princess Ingrid Alexandra, age 5, the future Queen of Norway.

Photo: Julia Marie Naglestad.
Courtesy Det Kongelige Hoff

King Harald V of Norway

Photo: Knut Kollandsrud.
Courtesy Det Kongelige Hoff

BIBLIOGRAPHY

Abels Kunstforlag. *Harald Prins av Norge* (Harald Prince of Norway). Oslo: Abels Kunstforlag, 1937.

Abels Kunstforlag. *Kronprincess Märthas Julealbum* (Crown Princess Märtha's Christmas Album). Oslo: Abels Kunstforlag, 1939.

Abels Kunstforlag. *Trekløveret på Skaugum* (The Three-leafed clover at Skaugum). Oslo: Abels Kunstforlag, 1938.

Aftenposten. "*Prins Haralds dåb*" (Prince Harald's Baptism). (March 31, 1937): 1.

Andenæs, Johs., O. Riste, and M. Skodvin. *Norway and Second World War.* Oslo: Aschehoug, 1996.

Benkow, Jo. *Olav: Menneske og Monark* (Olav: The Man and The Monarch). Oslo: Gyldendal Norsk Forlag, 1991.

Berg, Inga. "*Dagbok av Inga Berg 1937-1938*" (Journal of Inga Berg 1937-38).

Berg, John. Personal Interviews in Hønefoss, Norway, 2002-2004. Notes and photographs in possession of the author. John Berg is a nephew of Inga Berg and a son of Oddmund Berg, Inga's brother.

Berg, Marie. Postcard to Inga Berg, April 29, 1912. Picture Postcard of the ship *Olympic*, in possession of the author.

Bjerkness, Odell M. "The Future of the Monarchy: Early Life of Prince Harald." Edina, 2005.

Bomann-Larsen, Tor. *Folket: Haakon and Maud II* (The Nation: Haakon and Maud II). Oslo: Cappelens Forlag, 2004.

Brandt, Dr. Kr. *Lærebok for Jordmødre* (Textbook for Midwives). Kristiania: Aschehoug Forlag 1913.

Croft, Jennifer. *Exploring Careers in Midwifery.* New York: Rosen Publishing Group Inc, 1995.

Derry, T.K. *A History of St. Edmund's Church: 1884-1974.* Oslo: Merkantile Trykkeri, 1976.

Despard, Annabelle. Email interviews with the sister of Anita Despard in 2006- 2007; in possession of the author.

Dock, Lavinia L., R.N. *The Norwegian Council of Trained Nurses.* Copenhagen: Report to International Council of Nurses, 1922.

Eilers, Marlene A. *Queen Victoria's Descendents.* New York: Atlantic International Publications, 1937.

Gabrielson, Anne Marie and Per Gabrielson. Personal interviews in Bagn, Norway in 2004. Notes and photographs in possession of the author.

Gjermundsen, Jon Ola. *Gard og bygd i Sør-Aurdal, Bind A, Reinli og Vestre Bagn* (Farm and Community in South Aurdal, Vol. A, Reinli and West Bagn). Sør-Aurdal Kommune: Valdres Bygdebok Forlag, 1977.

Greve, Tim. *Haakon VII of Norway: The Man and the Monarch.* New York: Hippocrene Books, 1983.

Gyldendal Norsk Forlag. *Märtha: Norges Kronprinsesse 1929-1945: en Minnebok. Memory Book of Crown Princess Märtha, 1929-1945)* Oslo: Gyldendal Norsk Forlag, 1955.

Harriman, Florence Jaffray Hurst. *Mission to the North.* Philadelphia: J.B. Lippincott Co., 1945.

Haugstøl, Henrick. *Harald, Prins av Norge.* Oslo: Nasjonalhjelpen, 1948.

Hauge, Andreas and Knut Werner Hagen. *Bagn:1940.* Oslo: Forsvars Museet, 2001.

Herzstein, Robert Edwin. *Adolf Hitler and the German Trauma 1914-1945: An Interpretation of the Nazi Phenomenon.* New York: Perigee/G.P. Putnam's Sons, 1974.

Hegge, Per Egil. *Harald V en biografi.* Oslo: Damm and Søn, 2006.

Hjemmet (The Home). "*Haralds barnepike ga klokkestreng*" (Harald's Infant Nurse gave a Bellpull Hanging) [for the royal wedding]. no. 38, supplement to *Hjemmet*, (September 18, 1968).

Hjemmet. "Jeg var Kronprins Haralds Barnepike" (I was Crown Prince Harald's Nanny). no. 43, (1958): 34-42.

Hjemmet. "Skaugum: Her Skal De Bo" (Skaugum: Here They Shall Live). (1968)

Hybertson, Steinar. *Crown Princess Märtha: The American Story.* DVD. Seattle: Norwegian American Foundation, 2005.

Johnson, Amanda. *Norway, Her Invasion and Occupation.* Decatur, GA: Bowen Press, 1948.

Jordmorutdanningen: Gjordemor, Jordemor, Jordmor: 175 år Jordmorskolen i Oslo (Midwife Training: Midwife, Midwife, Midwife: 175 Years at the Midwife School in Oslo). Oslo: Jordmorutdanningen, 1993.

Killebrand, P., ed. *Valdres Bygebok* (Valdres Community Book). Vol. 4, 1954.

Kjæheim, Kristina. *Jordmorutdanning gjennom 175 år* (Midwifery education the past 175 years). Oslo: Trykk, 1990.

Larsson, Bergljot. "Norway's Nurses Carry on." *The American Journal of Nursing.* 46, No. 5 (May, 1945).

Lie, Nils D. *"Afgangsvidnesbyrd"* (School Graduation Report). Bagn Schools, April 28, 1906.

Melby, Kari. *Kall og Kamp: Norsk Sykepleierforbunds Historie* (Vocation and Struggle: History of the Norwegian Nurses Association). Oslo: J.W. Cappelens Forlag, 1990.

Midgaard, John. *A Brief History of Norway.* Oslo: Tano, 1986.

Møller, Arvid. *Kronprincess Märtha, Hustru-mor-medmenneske* (Crown Princess Märtha, Wife, Mother, Human Being). Oslo: J.W. Cappelens Forlag, A.S., 1990.

Nightingale, Florence. *Notes on Nursing: What It Is and What It Is Not.* Philadelphia: Lippincott, 1992.

Oppland Arbeiderblad (East Norway Workers News). *"Inga Berg fra Bagn Var Kronprinsens Barnepleierske"* (Inga Berg from Bagn was Crown Prince's Children's Nurse). (May 12, 1979): 13.

Oppland Arbeiderblad. "Inga fra Sør-Aurdal Var Barnepleierske for Arveprins Harald" (Inga from South Aurdal was Children's Nurse for Crown Prince Harald). No. 5 (February 4, 1983).

Princess Märtha Louise. *Why Kings and Queens Don't Wear Crowns.* Bloomington, MN: Skandisk, Inc., 2006.

Risåsen, Geir Thomas. *The Royal Palace.* Oslo: Andresen & Butenschøn, 2005.

Romansie, Joanne. "Look to Norway." *News of Norway.* Washington D.C.: Norwegian Embassy and Consulates General (Winter, 2005): 6-7.

Roesdahl, Else. *The Vikings.* London: Penguin Press Books, 1998.

Rosenlund, Arnfinn and Mary Ann Rosenlund. Personal interview on April 20, in 2007 in Edina, Minnesota. Notes are in possession of the author.

Skjervold, Christian Klebo II. "The Resistance Movement in Norway: World War II." M.A. Thesis, Minneapolis, University of Minnesota, June 1965.

Stenersen, Øivind and Ivar Libæk. *The History of Norway: From the Ice Age to Today.* Lysaker, Norway: Dinamo Forlag, 2003.

Tully, Grace. *F.D.R., My Boss.* New York: Charles Scribner's and Sons, 1949.

Wig, Kjell Arnljot. *Kongen Ser Tilbake* (The King Looks Back). Oslo: J.W. Cappelens Forlag, 1977.

Woxholth, Yngve, ed. *Kongeboliger og Nasjonalskatter i Norge* (Royal Residences and other National Treasures). Oslo: Hjemmes Forlag, 1978.

ILLUSTRATION AND PHOTO CREDITS

Abels Kunstforlag – pages 37, 40, 42, 43, 46, 51, 58, 61, 62, 63, 64, 65, 68, 69

Aftenposten – pages 33, 35, 37, 39, 59, 81, 82, 102

Johs. Andenaes – pages 75, 80

Aune Forlag – page 83

Jo Benkow – page 15

Inga Berg Collection   pages 1, 2, 28, 38, 39, 41, 43, 44, 46, 53, 70, 84

Odell Bjerkness Collection – pages 15, 18, 19, 20, 21, 23, 25, 28, 31, 73, 86, 102

Annabelle Despard – page 26

Elstad – page 62

Fritt Norge – pages 71, 80

Hjemmet – page 29

Det Kongelige Hoff – pages 102, 103

Lambert Projection – page 9

Magnus Magnussen – page 12

Kari Melby – page 26

Arvid Miller – pages 76, 77

Annemor Møst – pages 16, 17

Nasjonsbibliotek – pages 1, 24, 78, 81, 84

The Norseman – page 11

Norsk Ukeblad – page 29

Norwegian Resistance Museum   pages 70, 71

Arve Ragner – pages 51, 61, 70

Geir Thomas Risåsen – page 14

Sør- Aurdal – page 73

Vesterheim Genealogical Center – page 73

Yngve Woxholth – page 30

INDEX

Significant figures in bold, photographs in bold

SOURCES FOR SCANDINAVIAN LITERATURE

Skandisk, Inc. thanks the following stores, organizations, and websites that carry this book and other Scandinavian literature. Their support has made this edition of *The Prince and the Nanny* possible.

Al Johnson's Gift Shop
701 Bay Shore Drive
Sister Bay, WI 54234

Augsburg College Bookstore
610 22nd Ave S
Minneapolis, MN 55454

Bergquist Gift Shop
1412 S Highway 33 S
Cloquet, MN 55720

Bishop Hill Colony Store
101 West Main
Bishop Hill, IL 61419

BYU Bookstore
Brigham Young University
Provo, UT 84602

Books on Broadway
12½ West Broadway
Williston, ND 58801

Chapel in the Hills
3788 Chapel Lane
Rapid City, SD 57702

Distinctively Sweden
25 Messenger Street – Suite 1
Plaineville, MA 02762

Cobber Bookstore
Concordia College
Moorhead, MN 56562

Concordia Language Villages
9500 Ruppstrasse NE
Bemidji, MN 56601

Dregne's Scandinavian Gifts
100 S Main Street
Westby, WI 54667

Finn Ware of Oregon
1116 Commercial Street
Astoria, OR 97103

Garfield Book Co. at PLU
208 Garfield St – Suite 101
Tacoma, WA 98444

Gift Box
310 W State Street
Geneva, IL 60134

Hammer & Wikan
218 Nordic Drive
Petersburg, AK 99833

Heritage Shop – Hjemkomst
202 First Ave N
Moorhead, MN 56560

Heritage II
2183 3rd Street
White Bear Lake, MN 55110

Holsen Hus
126 S Phillips Ave
Sioux Falls, SD 57104

Ingebretsen's Scandinavian Gifts
1601 E Lake Street
Minneapolis, MN 55407

Joanne's Scandinavian Gifts
223 Rittenhouse Ave
Bayfield, WI 54814

Klaradal Swedish Antiques & Gifts
16644 Georgia Ave
Olney, MD 20832

Little Norway
3576 Hwy JG N
Blue Mounds, WI 53517

Little Scandinavia
2619 N Main Street
Elkhorn, NE 68022

Luther College Bookstore
700 College Drive
Decorah, IA 52101

MN Historical Museum Store
345 Kellogg Blvd W
St. Paul, MN 55102

www.nordichouse.com
Nordic Distributors
Oakland, CA 94609

Nordic Galleri
221 West Lincoln Ave
Fergus Falls, MN 56537

Nordic Heritage Museum
3014 NW 67th St
Seattle, WA 98117

Nordic Impressions
38 Bearskin Neck
Rockport, MD 01966

Nordic Maid
18954 C Front St
Poulsbo, WA 98370

Nordic Nook
176 W Main St
Stoughton, WI 53589

Nordic Shop
111 S Broadway – Suite 202
Rochester, MN 55904

www.NorseAmerica.com
Norseamerica, LLC
Atlanta, GA 30340

email: Norskmedia@aol.com
Norskmedia
Indialantic, FL 32903

Norwegian Seamen's Church
1772 Prytania St
New Orleans, LA 70130

Norwegian Seamen's Church
317 E 52nd St
New York, NY 10022

Norwegian Seamen's Church
4309 Young St
Pasadena, TX 77504

Norwegian Seamen's Church
2454 Hyde St
San Francisco, CA 94109

Norwegian Seamen's Church
1035 S Beacon St
San Pedro, CA 90731

Open House Imports
308 E Main St
Mt. Horeb, WI 53572

Punzel Scandinavian
8720 Cty Road 633
Buckley, MI 49620

Rasmussen's
1697 Copenhagen Dr
Solvang, CA 93463

www.ruralroutebookstore.com
Rural Route Bookstore
Grand Rapids, MN 55744

Saving Thyme
233 W Main St
Stoughton, WI 53589

Scandia Imports
10020 SW Beaverton Hills Hwy
Beaverton, OR 97005

Scandinavia Place
209 N Main
Independence, MO 64050

Scandinavian Affär
319 N 1st Ave
Sandpoint, ID 83864

Scandinavian Import Company
8669 N Main St
Helen, GA 30545

Scandinavian Heritage Museum
1020 S Broadway
Minot, ND 58701

Scandinavian Imports
16 S Barstow
Eau Claire, WI 54701

www.scandinavianmarket.com
Scandinavian Marketplace
Hastings, MN 55033

Scandinavian Specialties
6719 15th Ave NW
Seattle, WA 98117

www.scandinavian-touch.com
Scandinavian Touch
Lahaska, PA 18931

Scandinavian Trends
25 E Napa Street, C
Sonoma, CA 95476

Solbjorg's Norwegian Gifts
10677 N Bay Shore Drive
Sister Bay, WI 54234

Sons of Norway - Trollheim
9195 W Progress Place
Littleton, CO 80123

Stabo Scandinavian Imports
830 Kirkwood Mall
Bismarck, ND 58504

Stabo Scandinavian Imports
West Acres Shopping Center
Fargo, ND 58103

Stockholm Inn
2420 Charles St
Rockford, IL 61108

Strictly Scandinavian
3110 Harborview Drive
Gig Harbor, WA 98335

Svensk Butik
1465 Draper St
Kingsburg, CA 93631

Swedish Crafts
135 N Main St
Lindsborg, KS 67456

Swedish Passport Company
626 Iron St
Norway, MI 49870

Uffda Shop
202-204 Bush St
Red Wing, MN 55066

Valley Troll
1222 Granite St
Granite Falls, MN 56241

Vanberia International Gifts
217 W Water St
Decorah, IA 52101

Vesterheim Museum
502 W Water St
Decorah, IA 52101

Viking House
19 N Main St
Concord, NH 03301

Viking Treasures
438 R P Coffin Rd
Long Grove, IL 60047

Wooden Spoon
1617 K Ave
Plano, TX 75074